W9-CJW-234

TALES FROM
AUGUSTA'S FAIRWAYS

A COLLECTION OF THE GREATEST
MASTERS STORIES EVER TOLD

JIM HAWKINS

WITH ROBERT HARTMAN

SPORTS
PUBLISHING

To Mark,
who is mastering this baffling game
in a manner his father never could.

Sports Publishing books may be purchased in bulk at special discounts for sales promotion, corporate gifts, fund-raising, or educational purposes. Special editions can also be created to specifications. For details, contact the Special Sales Department, Sports Publishing, 307 West 36th Street, 11th Floor, New York, NY 10018 or sportspubbooks@skyhorsepublishing.com.

Sports Publishing® is a registered trademark of Skyhorse Publishing, Inc.®, a Delaware corporation.

Visit our website at www.sportspubbooks.com

10 9 8 7 6 5 4 3 2 1

Library of Congress Cataloging-in-Publication Data is available on file.

ISBN: 978-1-61321-079-6

Printed in the United States of America

Contents

1

Cathedral in the Pines

"The Masters is a monument to everything that is great in golf. It is a cut above. Way above."
— *Jack Nicklaus*

The first thing that strikes you, the first time you set foot on hallowed, immaculate Augusta National, is how utterly green everything is. How absolutely perfect.

Instantly, you can understand how Masters founder and amateur legend Bobby Jones felt, more than 70 years ago, when he first laid eyes on the paradise that would become Augusta National.

In his autobiography, *Golf Is My Game*, Jones wrote:

"When I walked out on the grass terrace under the big trees behind the house and looked down over the property, the experience was unforgettable. It seemed that this land had been lying here for years waiting for someone to lay a golf course upon it. Indeed, it looked as though it already were a golf course."

To this day, the breathtaking scene virtually explodes right before your eyes:

Majestic, carpet-like, rolling green fairways, framed by towering green loblolly pine trees, leading, of course, to impeccably manicured greens.

Then you notice the picturesque ponds, filled with reflections of flawless pink and white flowers, the caddies clad in their distinctive, snow-white coveralls, and the charming pine straw paths. There are 1,600 azaleas on hole No. 13 alone.

At the rear of the stately, steepled white clubhouse with black shutters—the first all-concrete structure erected in the South (when it was built in 1854 as a home for Dennis Redmond, who owned the thriving indigo plantation on the property at the time)—stands a 150-year-old oak tree.

Planted before the start of the Civil War, it is now three stories high, stretching 40 yards from limb to limb.

Before Bobby Jones, before Ben Hogan, before Arnold Palmer, before Jack Nicklaus, before Tiger Woods, that oak tree was there, overlooking what is now the first tee of the most famous, the most venerated golf course in the world.

There is no swimming pool at Augusta National. No tennis courts. Augusta National is not like other country clubs. There isn't even an annual club championship.

Exalted Augusta National is all about the Masters. Period.

You will find no billboards at Augusta National. No blimps flying overhead during the Masters. No skyboxes, no corporate hospitality chalets or tents.

No sponsor is wanted. Nor is one needed here.

Augusta National, where the quaint scoreboards are still operated by hand and where thousands of pimento cheese sandwiches are painstakingly wrapped year after year in green cellophane, doesn't simply exhibit tradition and nostalgia and class.

It exudes it.

Those indigo plants on Dennis Redmond's plantation produced berries that were the source of the dark blue dye that was used in the late 1800s to produce a popular new piece of apparel known as blue jeans.

Today, no one in the know would dare to wear blue jeans at dignified Augusta National.

The first Masters was played in late March, but the next year it was moved to April where, thanks to Augusta National's blooming azaleas, dogwoods, and rosebuds, the tournament soon became one of the traditional harbingers of spring—and the new golf season.

Many of the plants that bloom each April at Augusta are direct descendants of the flowers once featured at Fruitlands Nursery, which formerly flourished on the grounds.

When co-founder Clifford Roberts proposed moving the Masters to the first week in April in the late 1930s, an Augusta National club member noted: "The problem is, that means we'll finish on Easter Sunday."

"Well, who's in charge of scheduling Easter this year?" Roberts inquired. "We'll get them to move it."

Augusta National's dense hedges hide the peaceful patch of heaven from the prying eyes of uninvited passers-by on frenzied, fast-food filled Washington Road. A trip to the Masters truly is a trip back in time to a more genteel era when golf was primarily a game for a privileged, well-to-do few.

Each April, the gentlemen in green jackets open their gates and allow everyone lucky enough to land a ticket a peek into their private little paradise.

Once inside the sanctuary, people patiently stand in line for hours for the privilege of purchasing an official Masters shirt or cap to prove to friends back home that they actually were there.

Since the inaugural Masters in 1934, the familiar Augusta National map-and-flagstick logo has never varied.

Very few ardent golf enthusiasts follow the prestigious U.S. Open from venue to venue, year after year. But thousands—arguably, tens of thousands—return to Augusta National each April.

"The minute you drive in these gates, you begin to choke up," admitted Gary Player, who has conquered glorious Augusta National three times.

In the early years, sportswriters, heading home to the Northeast and Midwest after baseball's annual spring training in Florida, were happy to stop off in hospitable Augusta along the way.

That helped to promote the Masters. It also didn't hurt that Grantland Rice, the country's foremost sportswriter at the time and a nationally known celebrity, was one of Augusta National's most active, enthusiastic members.

Because of Jones' and Roberts' attention to detail, the Masters soon gained a reputation for being the best-run golf tournament in the world—a distinction that sets Augusta National apart to this day.

Masters spectators are called "patrons," not fans. The sand-filled hazards at the Masters are referred to as bunkers, not traps. The conveniently placed barrels are filled with "refuse," never garbage or trash.

The two halves of the storied golf course are referred to as "the first nine" and "the second nine," rather than "front" and "back," because Clifford Roberts— who added to the lore of Augusta by committing suicide in 1977 at age 84 on the adjacent par-3 course— believed the phrase "back side" sounded vulgar.

The Masters is, without a doubt, the toughest ticket in sports. Yet prices at Augusta National remain a fraction of what the market would bear.

Parking for patrons is free. Augusta National was the first course to provide complimentary parking on club grounds for 10,000 cars.

The Masters was also the first tournament to provide bleachers—or "observation stands," as Roberts called them—for the comfort of spectators. And it was the first golf tournament to be broadcast live from coast to coast on radio.

It was also the first to station up-to-the-minute scoreboards at various vantage points around the course, the first to use ropes to maintain order within the galleries, and the first to employ private detectives to oversee security.

Prices in the concession stands and souvenir tents have always been purposely kept low.

Daily pairings sheets that include a map of the course are given away to all who enter the grounds. There is no need to purchase expensive, bulky programs, although those also are available.

In the Augusta National pro shop, the staff makes change with new currency because Clifford Roberts wouldn't tolerate dirty, tattered bills.

In that way, too, the annual Masters is unlike any other major sporting event in the land.

According to legend, Spanish explorer Hernando de Soto, traveling through what is now the southern United States in search of treasure in the early 1500s, stopped at the site of Augusta National.

Early Georgia pioneers and Indian chiefs are said to have pow-wowed near the spring-fed pond that is part of Augusta's par-3 course.

During the Revolutionary War, a tavern stood on Washington Road, near Magnolia Lane and what is now the fabled main entrance to Augusta National.

The course was constructed on what had formerly been the 365-acre Fruitlands Nursery, owned and operated by a Belgian family headed by Prosper Julius Alphonse Berckmans, on what was then the outskirts of Augusta.

The property was filled with flowers and trees and shrubs. Sixty-two magnolia trees lined the narrow driveway that led to the Berckmans' plantation home on what had been the south's first commercial nursery.

After Berckmans passed away in 1910, Fruitlands Nursery slowly fell into a state of disrepair. In 1925, a Miami businessman sought to built a golf course and a $2 million hotel on the property, but went bankrupt soon after the project began.

It was Bobby Jones' friend, bespectacled Wall Street stockbroker and speculator Clifford Roberts, who first alerted Jones to the possibility of purchasing the abandoned Fruitlands Nursery for $75,000, or about $200 an acre.

Roberts had become acquainted with the picturesque property while he was stationed in Augusta during the final months of World War I.

It was Roberts, along with Jones, who convinced a number of well-to-do friends to invest in the project, even though the country was immersed in the Great Depression. Roberts himself had absorbed a financial pounding in the 1929 Crash.

And it was the meticulous perfectionist Roberts who ran Augusta National with an iron fist for the first 40 years.

Despite the affluence and prominence of its founders and original members, Augusta National was frequently in financial trouble during its early years.

The original business plan, as set forth by Jones and Roberts, called for 1,800 members with annual dues of $60. The founders planned to reduce that fee as soon as the new club became profitable.

Jones and Roberts also planned to build a second course, a "Ladies Course" for members' wives, as soon as the membership reached 1,000.

The two men distributed thousands of membership forms to people they presumed might be interested. Initially, all one had to do to join was fill out the index-card sized membership application and return it with a check. No approval was required.

But on the eve of the inaugural 1934 Masters, Augusta National had only 76 members.

Designed in the early 1930s by renowned golf course architect Alister Mackenzie, with Bobby Jones looking over his shoulder, prim and proper Augusta National is, indeed, golf's Mecca.

Mackenzie was hand-picked by Jones to design his dream course because both men shared the same philosophy toward the game.

Jones, who personally didn't believe in rough, insisted that Augusta National be challenging as well as a pleasure to play. He wanted a course that would "give pleasure to the greatest possible number of players without respect to their capabilities."

And Mackenzie, the Scotsman who had designed Cypress Point in California, sought to build courses that would provide "the most enjoyment for the greatest number."

A golfer once approached Mackenzie to tell him about a course he had recently played.

"It's very difficult," the golfer explained. "No one has ever broken par there."

"My goodness," Mackenzie replied, "what's wrong with it?"

Unfortunately, Mackenzie, who considered Augusta National his "finest achievement," never saw the finished product.

Following a trip to Scotland in 1933, he fell seriously ill and he died, virtually broke, in California in January, 1934—less than three months before the inaugural Masters.

At the time of his death, Mackenzie had been paid less than half of the $10,000 that he been promised for designing Augusta National.

Fifty-nine businessmen paid $350 apiece in the early 1930s to become charter members of the new golf club under construction in East Georgia.

The Masters—initially known as the Augusta National Invitation Tournament, because Jones thought

"Masters" sounded too presumptuous—was conceived as much to attract national attention and new members to Jones' club as it was to provide top-notch, world-class competition.

In the beginning, the Augusta National Invitation Tournament was meant to be merely a modest, informal get-together, a relaxed reunion of friends.

Jones would invite his golfing buddies as well the most prominent stars in the game, including the reigning champions of the U.S. and British Opens, the U.S. and British Amateurs, and the PGA championship, along with members of the U.S. Ryder Cup and Walker Cup teams.

Given the distinguished, all-star nature of the field, the term Masters was too apropos to ignore and the new title was quickly adopted.

Although all Masters champions immediately become honorary members of the club, they are never allowed to invite a guest to play Augusta National with them even during the off-season, unless that guest is accompanied by a bona fide club member.

In late 1935, banks actually began foreclosure proceedings against financially strapped Augusta National. Roberts once stated that if he and Jones had known the

Great Depression would last as long as it did, they never would have built the course.

It was not until 1939 that the Masters turned the corner and began to show a modest profit.

When Herman Keiser won the 1946 Masters, the first held after Augusta's World War II hiatus, he was informed that his plaque would be shipped as soon as the club could afford to purchase the silver necessary to make the trophy.

"While we may not have expected it originally," Clifford Roberts wrote, "we have created a tournament of such importance that we are bound to see that it continues."

In an effort to raise much-needed revenue, Augusta National tried for more than 20 years to sell or lease land bordering the golf course to members and prospective members interested in building homes nearby.

As incredible as it sounds today, only one such home was ever built, and as recently as the early 1950s Clifford Roberts couldn't even get Augusta real estate brokers to return his phone calls.

Before Roberts took his own life in 1977, he made certain that one home had been torn down.

Famed Magnolia Lane, the magical, narrow 330-yard driveway leading from Augusta National's main gate to the historic clubhouse, is flanked by 62 huge magnolia trees, planted before the Civil War, when boats hauled indigo and cotton from area plantations down the Savannah River to the Atlantic Ocean.

During Masters Week, only green-jacketed Augusta National members and participating golfers are permitted to traverse Magnolia Lane.

Uniformed Pinkertons silently stand guard at each end of the tree-canopied drive to make certain no one else dares to set foot on the sacred path.

Cameras are not permitted on the course during the tournament. Radios, TV sets, cellular phones, walkie-talkies, beepers, tape recorders, coolers, picnic baskets, flags, banners, periscopes, ladders, and stools are prohibited, too.

Fans—excuse me, "patrons"—annually arrive at the crack of dawn to stake out their places on the course, where they gladly spend the day, sitting on official green Masters collapsible chairs, politely applauding every shot by every golfer who passes by.

Those official green chairs are the only ones allowed on the golf course once the tournament begins. And they are only sold in the official Augusta National souvenir tent —and only during Masters week.

In addition, patrons are not supposed to ask for a player's autograph anywhere but in a narrow area near the participants' parking lot.

Today, would-be Augusta National members cannot apply. They must wait to be "invited."

In fact, you are not even supposed to express an eagerness in joining this most-exclusive club.

How much does it cost to join Augusta National?

If you have to ask, the members reason, you obviously do not belong.

Although such information remains a closely guarded secret, a membership at Augusta National reportedly now costs in the neighborhood of $40,000.

Members also understand that speaking about Augusta National to outsiders is frowned upon. Only the current Masters chairman is allowed to do that.

Away from Augusta National, members are not even permitted to boast about their own accomplishments on the storied course.

Former Masters winners dress in the Champions Locker Room. Actually, there aren't enough lockers for everyone, so many current players find themselves paired with former champions, some of whom have passed away.

Upstairs in the "Crows' Nest," the young amateurs are invited to make themselves at home.

Traditionally, sometime during Masters week, when no one is around, the amateurs try to sneak a peek into the sacred Champions Locker Room.

Tiger Woods did it. So did Jack Nicklaus.

Spectators are advised how, and when, to cheer.

Each day, each patron is given a free map of the golf course and a schedule of the day's tee times, which also carries the following admonition from Masters founder Bobby Jones:

"It is appropriate for spectators to applaud successful strokes in proportion to difficulty, but excessive demonstrations by a player or his partisans are not proper. . . . Most distressing to those who love the game of golf is the applauding or cheering of misplays or misfortunes of a player.

"Such occurrences have been rare at the Masters, but we must eliminate them entirely if our patrons are to continue their reputation as the most knowledgeable and considerate in the world."

Jones penned those words in 1967, after members of "Arnie's Army" cheered when Arnold Palmer's new rival, Jack Nicklaus, missed a putt.

In the entire kingdom of sports, only Augusta and the Masters still stand for the very same things they stood for nearly 70 years ago.

Three-time Masters champion Sam Snead, who still tees off in special ceremonies to start the tournament each April, declared: "If you asked golfers what tournament they would rather win over all the others, I think every one of them to a man would say, 'The Masters.'"

2

Tiger

———————

"I'm not great with golf history, but I'll tell you right now that in the past 100 years, no one is even on the same page as this kid."

— *Rocco Mediate*

It was entirely fitting, and perhaps ordained, that, in the 30th anniversary of the year that Masters' founder and national amateur hero Bobby Jones passed away, a young man named Eldrick T. Woods—who was born the same year that Lee Elder became the first black man ever permitted to compete in the Masters—should join Jones as just the second golfer in the history of the game to reign as champion of all four of the sport's greatest tournaments at the same time.

It simply doesn't get much more melodramatic than that, even in the magical land of Amen Corner and Rae's Creek.

"Some of the golfing gods must have been looking down on me," admitted Tiger Woods, minutes after he outdueled David Duval and Phil Mickelson in a pressure-packed shoot-out to win the 2001 Masters by two strokes and wrap up his unprecedented, slightly asterisked version of golf's modern Grand Slam.

"I don't think I can ever accomplish anything that would top this," Tiger said.

Of course, nothing Tiger Woods accomplishes at storied Augusta National from now on will come as a surprise after what he has already done.

No one—not Gene Sarazen, not Sam Snead, not Arnold Palmer, not even Jack Nicklaus—has ever turned Augusta National upside-down the way Tiger has.

"I've cried after wins and I've cried after defeats," admitted Woods, who first stunned the golf world as a 21-year-old by lapping the illustrious field to win the 1997 Masters with a record score (270) and by a record 12 strokes.

"But I've never had a feeling like this before," Tiger said moments after his historic 2001 Masters triumph. "It's a weird feeling."

Woods' father, Earl, placed a sawed-off golf club in the infant's crib and had Tiger hitting balls from his walker before he could stand up on his own two feet.

By age 2, little Eldrick was playing golf. At age 3, Tiger had already played nine holes—and shot a 45. At 4, he had appeared on national TV.

Young Woods recorded his first hole-in-one when he was 8. His playing partner had to lift little Tiger up into the air so he could see that the ball had disappeared into the hole.

Woods was the youngest man ever to win the U.S. Junior Amateur Championship (15), the youngest to win the U.S. Amateur (18), and the youngest to win the Masters (21 years, 3 months, 14 days).

Tiger accomplished something in April, 2001, that no one—with the possible exception of Woods himself—may ever accomplish again.

With the whole world watching his every shot, Woods withstood an onslaught of eight birdies by the hard-charging David Duval to complete his 12-month, 4-for-4 sweep of golf's grandest events.

Tiger Woods

So what if a New Year's Eve celebration intervened?

Even the normally unflappable Woods was momentarily taken aback by the magnitude of what he had just done. He buried his face in his cap for a moment, demonstrating he is, indeed, human after all.

"I sort of lost it a little bit," Tiger confessed. "I put my cap over my face and tried to get it back together.

"When you're out there focusing, grinding it out, you don't really have time to think about the peripheral things. I had focused so hard on every shot all day. I was in such a zone. After I made my birdie putt on 18, I suddenly realized it was over. I was done.

"I thought to myself, 'I don't have any more shots to hit. I've won the Masters.' "

Woods' 2000-01 Grand Slam ranks among sport's all-time great feats, along with Joe DiMaggio's 56-game hitting streak in 1941, Byron Nelson's 11-tournament winning streak in 1945, Walter Payton's 16,726 career rushing yards, and Bill Russell's 11 NBA titles in 13 years.

"I'm not great with golf history," said fellow pro Rocco Mediate, who stuck around long after his own round was over that historic Sunday at the 2001 Masters to watch the traditional late-afternoon green jacket ceremonies, "but I'll tell you right now that in the past 100 years, no one is even on the same page as this kid."

The inevitable expectation of victory, and the overwhelming need to win—each time, every time, all the time —gnawed at golf greats such as Bobby Jones and Byron Nelson and eventually drove them both from the competitive game.

On the other hand, Tiger Woods seems to thrive on the pressure and pandemonium that many others have found so ponderous.

Tiger needs pressure to kindle his inner fires. The bigger the challenge, the better he likes it.

That is what separates Woods from Jones—and also from so many of Tiger's contemporaries.

"It's not life or death," Woods explained. "It's fun."

With what could arguably be labeled golf's greatest feat in 71 years on the line, the interest and excitement surrounding the 2001 Masters neared an all-time high.

Before the tournament began, coveted week-long spectator badges, with a face-value $125, were reportedly being sold on the black market out on hectic Washington Road for between $5,500 and $7,000 apiece.

Requests for press credentials increased by 25 percent. Reporters flew into tiny Augusta from Japan, England, Ireland, Scotland, Italy, Spain, Germany and the Czech Republic.

Oddly enough, one country that didn't dispatch a reporter to Augusta was Fiji, birthplace of defending Masters champion Vijay Singh.

The 2001 Masters was carried on TV in 190 countries, including non-golfing hot-beds such as Indonesia, Panama, Iceland, Liechtenstein, and Namibia.

All of which merely seemed to whet Woods' appetite for action.

"I absolutely enjoy coming out here and competing and playing," Woods gushed before the tournament began. "I love it!

"It's such a big kick for me as a player. I love to be able to put myself in contention, coming down the stretch on the back nine, and have to execute a golf shot.

"Your nerves are fluttering, your eyeballs are beating, your palms are sweating—it's fun to be able to experience that, and somehow be able to control it and pull off a shot."

Never has a player, any player, won all four of golf's modern major tournaments—the Masters, U.S. Open, British Open and PGA Championship—in the same year.

Only five golfers—Gene Sarazen, Ben Hogan, Gary Player, Jack Nicklaus, and now Woods—have ever won all four at any time whatsoever during their distinguished careers.

And only Woods and Hogan have ever managed to win as many as three of those majors in the same season.

Until 1930, no one ever mentioned such a thing as a "Grand Slam." No one even imagined that such a feat was possible.

Golf, in the first half of the last century, was dominated by amateurs. The U.S. Open, U.S. Amateur, British Open, and British Amateur reigned as the game's most prestigious events. Until 1934 there was no Masters. And the PGA Championship was small potatoes.

Unbeknownst to all but a few, in 1926 Bobby Jones had privately set his sights on just such an sweep. The man who would later found Augusta National and the Masters, revealed his goal to Atlanta sportswriter O.B. Keeler, then swore him to secrecy.

After Jones won the U.S. and British Opens as well as the Amateur championships in both countries in 1930, Keeler borrowed a phrase from the country club card game of bridge and began trumpeting Jones' achievement as a "Grand Slam."

In 1997, 21-year-old Tiger Woods was not yet a champion, but no longer a longshot. In fact, he was a Masters pre-tournament favorite.

In anticipation, Augusta National received nearly 500 more media requests than usual that year. Ticket prices on the black market soared as high as $8,000 for the week. One ticket broker, unable to fulfill all of the orders he had accepted, committed suicide.

Estimates placed the tournament crowd at 42,000 per day.

By Sunday's final round, Tiger was out of sight of the rest of the field. Woods spent Saturday evening eating fast food and playing video games and Ping-Pong with friends at his rented home.

He tried to organize a pick-up basketball game, but his coach, Butch Harmon—son of 1948 Masters champion Claude Harmon—quickly squelched that idea.

Woods took a nine-stroke lead to the first tee on Sunday afternoon in 1997 and shot a Masters-record four-round score of 270, 18 under par, to outdistance the competition by 12 strokes, another record. In all, he shattered 20 Masters records and tied six others that year.

En route to victory, Woods posted two eagles, a dozen birdies and no bogies on the critical, often-decisive back nine.

On every hole, he was greeted by a standing ovation. It was the most-watched golf telecast in history.

Tiger Woods had arrived.

Jack Nicklaus, owner of six green jackets himself, was so impressed he immediately predicted Woods would own at least nine more green Masters jackets before his career was over.

"If I can keep putting myself there (in contention) for the next, whatever it is, 15, 20, 30 years, I'll win my share," Tiger predicted.

Ironically, Woods' 1997 Masters triumph occurred the same week major league baseball was commemorating the 50th anniversary of Jackie Robinson's historic breakthrough as the first black participant in that sport.

Woods, who is besieged with demands for his autograph wherever he goes, claims he never asked a celebrity for a signature when he was a kid.

"Never," insists Tiger. "I always thought autographs should be on checks. That's where they're most important."

Tiger Woods is allergic to azaleas. Each April in Augusta, most golfers are allergic to him.

The mere sight of Woods' name on the Masters' leader board is sufficient to strike fear in the hearts of many of his rivals.

But has Woods ever been intimidated himself?

Just once.

"It was the first and only time I was intimidated on a golf course," Tiger recalled, prior to the 2000 Masters.

"I was 11 years old and playing this 12-year-old in the Junior World Championship, and I had a chance to win if I played a good solid round. There was a 290-yard, par-4, and he drove the green. At 12 years old, he drove the green!

"I was really taken a little aback by that," Woods admitted. "I felt there was no way I could compete, no way I could win.

"I ended up beating him and almost winning the tournament. My dad and I talked about it later. He said, 'If you've put in the hard work, there is no point in being intimidated on the golf course.'"

3

The Bear

"The Masters without Jack Nicklaus is like your wife losing the diamond out of her wedding ring. Jack really put the Masters on the map. Jack is the Masters. He's it."
— *Greg Norman*

In the beginning, they called him "Ohio Fats" and "Baby Beef."

Chubby-cheeked Jack Nicklaus, who won his first Masters in 1963 at the age of 23—the youngest champion ever up until that time—and eventually won a record five more green jackets, was not exactly a favorite of most Masters' fans in the beginning.

Arnold Palmer was their hero, their beloved.

But the "Golden Bear," the 205-pound blond bomber who had trumpeted his arrival on the highest level of the game by besting Palmer in a playoff to win the 1962 U.S. Open, eventually won the galleries over with his class and his dominating play.

Nicklaus was, in fact, the annual favorite, or among the favorites, to win the Masters for 20 years in a row.

No one, including Arnie, ever ruled golf's most storied tournament the way Nicklaus did.

No one, until Tiger Woods, that is—and Tiger still has a long way to go to match Jack.

In the four years from 1963-66, Nicklaus won the Masters three times and finished second behind four-time winner Arnold Palmer once.

In all, Nicklaus has won six green jackets and finished second four times. It doesn't get much better than that.

To Jack Nicklaus, the Masters was always the tournament that mattered most.

"The Masters has a mystique about it," Nicklaus explained. "The mystique about Augusta National is Bob Jones and what he meant to golf, the class with which the event is held, all the special things that you just don't find other places."

In 1963, Nicklaus sank a three-foot putt on 18 to win at Augusta National for the first time, outdistancing Sam Snead, Julius Boros and Tony Lema.

"I'm not sure how long that putt was," Nicklaus admitted. "I closed my eyes."

Two years later, Nicklaus crushed arch-rival Palmer, Gary Player and Augusta National, with a resounding four-round score of 271—a record not topped until Tiger Woods took the storied tournament by storm in 1997.

Many labeled Nicklaus' dramatic 1975 victory over Johnny Miller, who was being hailed as "the new Nicklaus," and Tom Weiskopf, who had recently regained his old confidence, the best Masters ever.

"In all the time I've played golf, this is the most exciting day I've ever had," Nicklaus himself declared.

Weiskopf, who was forced to settle for runner-up honors at Augusta for the fourth time, later admitted that dramatic 1975 loss effectively ended his competitive career.

Who can ever forget 46-year-old Nicklaus' turn-back-the-clock final round 65, including a sizzling 30 on the back nine, that earned Jack his record sixth green jacket in 1986?

"I finally found that guy I used to know on the golf course," Nicklaus, who rallied from six shots behind with 10 holes to play, informed his wife Barbara. "It was me."

What made that remarkable victory even more special was the fact that Nicklaus' son, Jackie, caddied for him that week.

"I was so proud of him," the younger Nicklaus said later. "When he putted out on 18, I told him: 'Dad, I loved seeing you play today. It was the thrill of my lifetime. I mean, that was awesome.'"

Then, golfer and caddie, father and son, strolled off the golf course, with their arms around one another.

Many people believed Nicklaus was over the hill by 1986. After all, he hadn't won a major since 1980, or a tournament of any kind since 1984. And many members of the media didn't hesitate to point those depressing facts out.

Even CBS analyst Ken Venturi was heard to wonder aloud: "Jack's got to start thinking about when it's time to retire."

One of Nicklaus' close friends posted a copy of one such disparaging article on the refrigerator of Jack's rented home in Augusta that week.

"All week, I kept thinking: 'Done, through, washed up, huh?' " Nicklaus admitted.

On Thursday's opening round, faced with 11 putts of 15 feet or less, Nicklaus made only one.

"If I could just putt," Nicklaus mused the next morning, "I just might scare somebody. Maybe me."

But after Nicklaus shot himself into contention with a third-round 69 on Saturday, his son, Steve, phoned.

"Well, Pop," Steve Nicklaus asked, "what's it going to take?"

"Sixty-six will tie and 65 will win," The Bear predicted.

"Well," Steve replied, "go ahead and do it."

Then Nicklaus went out on Sunday and shot a 65 to overtake Greg Norman, Seve Ballesteros and Tom Kite.

Jack Nicklaus

Augusta's huge galleries were solidly behind Nicklaus Sunday as the 46-year-old fans' favorite made his gallant charge.

"The sound, walking from green to tee, was actually deafening," Nicklaus said, appreciatively.

As Nicklaus walked from the 15th green, where he had just scored an eagle with a 12-foot putt, to the 16th tee, the crowd went wild.

"I knew I had to make that putt if I wanted to have a chance to win," Nicklaus later confided.

"I couldn't hear anything, I mean, nothing!" he declared. "All I knew was that I was putting the ball on the green and making birdies, and I was going to keep doing it."

"I had tears in my eyes several times," Jack admitted. "I had to shake it off and tell myself, 'Hey, you've got some golf left to play.'"

After the '86 tournament, Tom Weiskopf was asked if he could imagine what must have been going through Nicklaus' mind en route to his record sixth Masters victory.

"If I knew what was going through Jack Nicklaus' head, I would have won this golf tournament," Weiskopf said.

In 1998, although he finished in a tie for sixth, four shots behind Mark O'Meara, the 58-year-old Nicklaus scored a victory for everyone with creaking bones and aching joints.

For a few exciting hours that sunny Sunday afternoon, it was 1986 all over again. It was vintage Jack Nicklaus, surging from back in the pack on the final round to catch the youngsters by surprise.

Nicklaus, who by then was pondering the end of his brilliant career, almost made it. As Nicklaus sank each of his six birdie putts, you could hear the roars all across the gorgeous golf course.

Jack simply ran out of holes—not heart.

"Every time I think I'm washed up, and everyone else does, too, I seem to play a little better," Nicklaus said, after his final-round 68.

As Nicklaus prepared to play the par-5 15th hole, he found himself thinking "eagle, eagle, birdie, birdie." Instead, he finished with a birdie and three pars.

"It was there," said Nicklaus, "if I had made the right shots. I had a chance the last three holes to make birdies and I missed all three of them. If I had made at least two of them I might have been in the hunt."

Same ol' Golden Bear.

"I'd be pretty stupid to say I wasn't thrilled," said Nicklaus. "But I'd be dishonest to say I wasn't disappointed. To finish four shots behind with the number of chances I gave away during this week hurts. Nothing is as emotional as winning. This was emotional but in a different way. Because I know I might never be here this way again."

"It's pretty neat," said Tiger Woods, when asked about Nicklaus' performance. "To see him right up there on the scoreboard where he used to be. It's pretty nostalgic. Especially being as old as he is.

"He is the standard, the best of all time," Woods declared. "I am proud to say Jack is my role model."

In 1971-72, Jack Nicklaus had a shot at holding all four major trophies at the same time, a la Tiger Woods.

In 1971, the PGA Championship was held first and Nicklaus won it. He did not win another major the rest of that year, but in '72—when the PGA reverted to its traditional late-summer status—Nicklaus won the Masters and U.S. Open, before bowing to Lee Trevino in the British Open by a single stroke.

In 1978, quite by coincidence, Nicklaus and Tom Weiskopf showed up at the course wearing identical outfits—navy blue pants, white shirts, and white shoes—for the final round.

While both golfers were on the putting green, a man walked up to Weiskopf and introduced himself as an FBI agent.

"We need to tell you that Jack has had a death threat," the agent said. "We don't think it's anything serious, but we have to take it very seriously, and you need to know this. I'll be walking very close to you guys, Jack will have another guy and we'll have people all through the gallery today. So don't get too concerned."

But, of course, Weiskopf was concerned—very concerned.

He grabbed his wife, Jeanne and said, "Please go to the pro shop and buy me something like a powder blue shirt."

By the time Weiskopf's wife returned, package in hand, the two players were on the first tee, ready to begin play. There was no time to return to the clubhouse to change.

"I took my shirt off and put on this powder blue shirt," Weiskopf recalled. "Everybody whistled and kind of 'oohed' and 'aahed'.

"Jack came over and said, 'What are you doing?'

"I said, 'I just want to make sure they don't shoot the wrong guy.'"

No tournament gives away more trophies and hardware than the Masters. And no golfer has won more trophies and awards (88) at Augusta National than Nicklaus.

Jack's collection of Augusta goodies includes:

Six sterling silver replicas of the Masters Trophy

One silver-gold cup

Seven gold medals

Five silver medals

Five silver cigarette boxes engraved with the players' names

One silver cigarette box engraved with the amateurs' names

One engraved silver tray

Forty-five crystal goblets

One crystal highball glass

Fifteen crystal vases

One silver salver

4

White Castles and Green Coats

"The Masters jacket epitomizes perfection in golf."
— *Gary Player*

Nothing is more synonymous with Augusta National and the Masters than the custom-tailored, Kelly-green, brass-buttoned, single-breasted jackets, introduced in 1937 so spectators would know whom to ask for assistance or information on the golf course.

Initially, the traditional, treasured coats—the color of Augusta's famed, well-manicured fairways—could be worn only by dues-paying members of the exclusive club.

But, beginning with Sam Snead in 1949, green jackets have also been presented to the winning golfer each year.

For the record, they are a tropical weight 50-50 blend of wool and polyester with a rayon lining, brass buttons on the front, and the Augusta National insignia on the left breast, and on the buttons, too.

No one is allowed to wear his distinctive green coat away from the course—although champions are permitted to take their jackets home for one year, provided they only wear them to golf-related events.

Except for Masters Week, the coats hang in a large cedar closet in the clubhouse.

No one is allowed to wear his Masters coat when making a commercial or engaging in any other mercenary endeavor.

When Gary Player neglected to return his 1961 green jacket in a timely manner, Clifford Roberts called Player's home in South Africa.

"He said, 'Gary, I believe you've taken the Masters jacket home,'" Player recalled. "'Nobody has been allowed to do that.'"

"You realize you're a member of one of the most exclusive groups of people in the world," observed Snead.

Multiple winners such as Tiger Woods, Jack Nicklaus, Arnold Palmer, Nick Faldo and Snead, only get one jacket.

As the conclusion of each tournament nears, several existing jackets that might fit the eventual winner are readied for the presentation ceremonies. Later, the new champion is measured for his own green coat.

Traditionally, the previous year's winner slips the green jacket over the shoulders of the new champion.

But in 1966, Jack Nicklaus became the first player to win back-to-back Masters.

"We have decided," Bobby Jones informed Jack, "that you will have to put the green jacket on yourself."

"That green coat," noted Chi Chi Rodriguez, who has never won one, "makes you choke."

It is the duty of the defending Masters champion to select the menu for the annual, exclusive, mid-week Past Champions Dinner.

In 2001, Vijay Singh, a native of Fiji, ordered Thai food, including spicy shrimp and chicken satay, chicken phanaeng kai and baked sea bass with chili sauce.

Out of sympathy for some of the older, former winners, Singh asked the chef to turn down the volume on the traditionally hot and spicy Thai cuisine.

Singh enjoys chicken phanaeng kai so much that Charlie Niyomkul, who owns the Tamarind Thai restaurant in Atlanta, made the 300-mile round trip to Augusta every day during the 2000 Masters to deliver Vijay's dinner.

Each former winner who attends the annual Past Champions Dinner receives a $5,000 honorarium from Augusta National.

But, in addition to selecting the menu, the defending champ is expected to pick up the check for the dinner.

"I would've paid a million bucks if I had to," admitted 1979 winner Fuzzy Zoeller. "That night is priceless."

Nick Faldo

In 1990, England's Nick Faldo served shepherd's pie along with fish and chips. Fuzzy Zoeller ordered White Castles for the main course in 1980.

Texan Ben Crenshaw imported BBQ—45 pounds of ribs, 30 pounds of sausage, 25 pounds of brisket and 60 14-ounce bottles of hot sauce—from his hometown of Austin. The feast was preceded by jalapeno pepper appetizers.

"I guess they look like pickles," Crenshaw later recalled. "Jack (Nicklaus) picked up a big one and popped it in before any of us could stop him. I will tell you, he was hurtin'. There was sweat pouring off of him."

Tiger Woods treated his peers to cheeseburgers, grilled chicken sandwiches, French fries and a milkshakes after his landslide 1997 victory.

Jose Maria Olazabal of Spain featured tapas, paella and hake, a white fish. Germany's Bernhard Langer ordered Black Forest torte and Wiener schnitzel. Mark O'Meara served sashimi and sushi as an appetizer

Nineteen eighty-eight champion Sandy Lyle, chose the traditional Scottish dish, haggis, which is made by mincing the heart, liver, and lungs of a sheep with onion and herbs, then boiling the mixture in a sheep's stomach.

Before the former champions began dining, Lyle pulled a dagger out of its sheath and performed the ceremonial stabbing of the haggis.

Dwight Eisenhower was a frequent visitor to Augusta National during his days as President of the United States.

Secret service agents, obliged to accompany Ike on the golf course, often carried Thompson submachine guns instead of clubs in their golf bags.

In 1953, the club added a cottage, known as the Eisenhower Cabin. The second floor included observation stations for Secret Service marksmen.

At Augusta National, no detail is too minute. Groundskeeper use soapy water to control mole crickets and hot water to control fire ants.

Inside the sacred Champions Locker Room, off-limits to both the public and the press, recent winners are expected to share cubicles with past champions.

Wherever possible, current players are paired with Masters winners who are either deceased or no longer participate.

When Augusta National doubled its total payout from $5,000 to $10,000 in 1946, the Masters also became the first golf tournament ever to charge $5 a day for a ticket.

In 1947, the Masters' galleries averaged only 5,000 patrons per day.

Only at the Masters do more people—thousands more—show up for the practice rounds early in the week than for the actual tournament, Thursday through Sunday.

That's because, for many of those fans, that is the only time they are able to get into Augusta National.

For years, people not fortunate enough to be on the annual badge list, could simply walk up to the gate and buy tickets for any of the Masters' three practice rounds.

But by 1994, the practice rounds themselves had become so popular that the crowds often reached the unmanageable level of 85,000 a day.

Now fans must apply much in advance and are subject to a lottery. The black market rate even for practice round tickets has been known to reach $300 a day.

The Masters never announces actually attendance figures—in the struggling, early years Clifford Roberts preferred to make the press guess, knowing full well their estimates would invariably be on the high side—but reportedly only 25,000 badges are sold for Thursday-thru-Sunday play, while between 40,000 and 50,000 practice-round tickets are now available each day.

The tournament has been sold out since 1966, and the list of those waiting to buy badges is so long that Augusta National stopped adding new names 24 years ago.

At the current rate of attrition, it will take club officials 30 years to catch up.

Incredibly, Augusta National is closed for maintenance and repairs from late May until mid-October—the height of the golf season in most other parts of the country.

In 1949, ropes were used at Augusta National for the first time to keep the galleries in check.

It wasn't until 1968 that the players with the highest scores teed off first on Sunday and the tournament leaders went off last.

Prior to 1957, there was no cut after 36 holes. From 1957 through 1961, the low 40 scores, plus ties, made the cut. Beginning in 1962, the low 44 and ties, along with anyone within 10 shots of the lead, qualified for the final 36 holes.

In November, 1937, Augusta National hosted the first national championship for professional players, 55 or older—forerunner to today's PGA Senior Tour.

The winner of inaugural senior championship was Jock Hutchinson. The following year, the tournament was won by Fred McLeod

The tournament was then relocated to Florida, but Hutchinson and McLeod—both of whom competed in the Masters until 1959—served as the Masters' first honorary starters in 1963.

Gene Sarazen and Byron Nelson resumed the custom in 1981, after a four-year hiatus. Ken Venturi served as a starter in 1983 when Nelson was ailing. Sam Snead joined the illustrious group in 1984.

5

The King

"He (Arnold Palmer) makes Willie Sutton look like Shirley Temple, the way he keeps stealing these golf tournaments."

— *Ken Venturi*

At Augusta National, Arnold Palmer truly was "The King."

Palmer personified the Masters from 1958 through 1967, winning four times, and only once finishing out of the top four.

It was at Augusta that Arnie's Army was born in '58 when Palmer won his first green jacket. The others quickly came in 1960, 1962, and 1964.

Palmer had the charisma, the flair, the personality, and the game that galleries—and the new television audience—loved.

"They cheer louder for him here than anywhere else," Tom Watson once noted. "I've never heard cheers like that. I can understand why. He's the man who made our game what it is."

Often with a cigarette hanging out his mouth, Arnie would tug at the glove on his left hand, hitch up his trousers, and hit shots few others would dare try.

With hair tousled and his shirt-tail hanging out, Arnie would charge down the fairway, much to his Army's delight.

"Go get 'em, Arnie!" they'd shout as Palmer attacked the course.

Airplanes towing banners reading, "Go, Arnie, Go," circled in the air above the golf course. On the ground fans followed him from hole to hole, round after round, shouting his name.

"Arnold Palmer," comedian Bob Hope quipped, "is the biggest crowd-pleaser since the invention of the portable sanitation facility."

At Augusta National, Palmer could do no wrong. And even when he did, no one seemed to care.

In 1960, apparent Masters winner Ken Venturi, who had finished with a final-round 70 and a four-day total of 283, was being interviewed by reporters when a roar suddenly went up out on the golf course.

"That's Palmer's gallery," one of the writers announced.

The smile immediately vanished from Venturi's face.

Someone rushed in from the golf course. "Palmer just holed it from all the way across the green for a birdie at 17!" he shouted, out of breath.

"Whoops," Venturi said, as he walked away.

Palmer had, in fact, holed a 27-footer on No. 17, and followed that with another birdie from five feet on the 18th, after a gutsy 6-iron shot from the fairway, to edge Venturi by a single stroke.

The huge gallery went wild. Their hero had done it again!

Palmer made his first trip to Augusta National in 1955 when he was a first-year professional and the reigning U.S. Amateur champ.

Arnie and his late wife, Winnie, traveled with a small camper, which they hooked up to the electricity and water in an Augusta trailer park. To save money,

Arnold Palmer

that was where they stayed during the tournament. They paid $11 for the week.

"I remember like it was yesterday the feeling as I drove up Magnolia Lane into Augusta National Golf Club for the first time," Palmer later wrote in his 1999 autobiography. "I'd never seen a place that looked so beautiful, so well manicured, and so purely devoted to golf, as beautiful as an ante-bellum estate, as quiet as a church.

"I remember turning to Winnie, who was as excited as I was, and saying quietly, 'This has got to be it, Babe.' Privately, I admitted to Winnie that it was like dying and going to heaven."

Others, however, were not nearly so impressed with young Arnie at first.

Palmer had earned his invitation to the Masters by winning the U.S. Amateur championship. Soon after he had settled into the clubhouse, Jackie Burke Jr. asked the 24-year-old Arnie if he would like to join him and Ben Hogan for a practice round.

Palmer, of course, eagerly accepted. But after watching Palmer scramble for three holes, Hogan turned to Burke and inquired: "How in hell did this guy get in the tournament?"

In 1961, Palmer, who won $696 for finishing 10th in his first Masters in 1955, found himself short of cash at lunch and had to borrow a dollar from Sam Snead to tip the clubhouse waiter.

"Why don't you ask Sam for his blood?" amateur Don Cherry suggested. "He'd rather part with that than a dollar."

The Era of Arnie at Augusta National dawned in 1958 when Palmer won his first of four Masters.

"This," Palmer declared after watching defending champion Doug Ford and Fred Hawkins both miss makeable birdie putts at 18, "is the greatest thrill of my life, bar none."

But Palmer's 1958 victory was marred somewhat by a rules controversy, and a prolonged debate over whether on not Arnie was entitled to a free drop on the 12th hole.

Palmer played two balls on that hole—one assuming a free drop, and one assuming a penalty.

A "5" had already been posted on the scoreboards when tournament officials decided Palmer was, indeed, entitled to a free drop and thus a "3" on that hole.

Some sportswriters later unfairly labeled Palmer a "rule book champion."

Jokester Jimmy Demaret, himself a three-time Masters champion, was watching the 1958 tournament on TV in the clubhouse when Arnold Palmer hit his tee shot to the back of the green on the par-3 16th hole.

"There's no way he gets down in two from there," Demaret loudly predicted.

When Palmer chipped in for a birdie-2, Demaret turned to his audience and said: "See, I told you."

After winning the 1958 Masters, and the $11,250 first prize that went with the green jacket, Palmer was so excited he accidentally added an extra zero and wrote his caddie a check for $14,000—when he actually meant to pay him $1,400.

As soon as Arnie discovered his costly error, he tracked his caddie down and requested a mulligan.

Masters champions are allowed to play Augusta National whenever they wish for the rest of their lives.

But that's where the club draws the line.

After Palmer won for the first time in 1958, he proudly brought his father, Deacon, down to Augusta to play a round.

"We're glad to have you play anytime you like," Clifford Roberts informed Arnie, after pulling him aside. "But your father can't play unless he has a member with him. That's one of our rules."

In 1962, Palmer finished birdie-birdie-par to force a three-way 18-hole playoff where he finished off Gary Player and Dow Finsterwald.

Although Arnie lost to Art Wall Jr. in 1959 and Gary Player in 1961 the legend—and Augusta's love affair with Palmer—continued to grow.

Palmer often cringed when he was paired with animated Chi Chi Rodriguez, the course clown.

In 1963, Masters officials asked Rodriguez to tone down his act at Augusta and stop doing the "Twist" after holing a putt.

"I like Chi Chi very much, and nobody likes to clown around or joke more on the course than I do," Palmer explained. "But there is a time and a place for it. In a tournament that has the dignity of the Masters, it should at least be spread out."

In 2000, Palmer became the first full-fledged Augusta National member in the modern era to also play in the tournament.

Actually, all former Masters champions are honorary members, permitted to play the course at any time.

Talk of a "Grand Slam" was rekindled in 1960, when   Palmer won the Masters and the U.S. Open

Once again it was a sportswriter, Bob Drum of Pittsburgh—Palmer's answer to Bobby Jones' O.B. Keeler—who resurrected the idea.

"I said, 'Wouldn't it be unique to have a Grand Slam of Golf?'" Palmer recalled. "Bob wrote about it and it's gone on from there."

Palmer was relaxing in the clubhouse before the final round of the 1966 Masters when young Raymond Floyd noticed the blue cap Arnie was wearing.

"You look funny in a cap," Floyd chided.

"I'm glad I have to wear a cap to look funny," Palmer shot back.

"Another couple of years and you're going to need all kinds of caps," Floyd continued. "You're going to need a transplant of hair from me."

Palmer took note of Floyd's thick, wavy locks and replied: "At least I don't have to put mine up in curlers."

President Dwight D. Eisenhower was a friend of Bobby Jones and Clifford Roberts and for years was a frequent visitor to Augusta National.

In 1972, as Arnold Palmer was preparing for his opening round, Ike's widow, Mamie, gave Arnie a good-luck kiss on the cheek on the porch of the Eisenhower Cabin.

"Do your darnedest," she said.

Palmer proceeded to shoot an opening-round 70.

At his first Masters, in 1985, Jose Maria Olazabal found himself paired with Palmer.

"That was the most people I'd ever seen on a golf course," recalled Olazabal, who shot 81-76 and missed the cut. "Everything he (Palmer) did, they clapped. I was just along for the ride."

6

Smile, You're on TV

"I hear we're on color TV today." — Doug Sanders, explaining his ensemble of yellow slacks, a yellow shirt and yellow shoes.

Many observers claim the 1953 Masters, won by Ben Hogan, marked the annual tournament's arrival as a true "major," on a par with the U.S. and British Opens and the PGA Championship.

Others insist it was the 1954 Masters—when Sam Snead bested Hogan in a playoff to win the tournament, which Bobby Jones himself labeled , "the greatest Masters ever"—that marked the turning point.

Certainly, no one can deny that it was during the 1950s and '60s that the Masters and Augusta National claimed center stage.

The era's Big Three, Arnold Palmer, Jack Nicklaus and Gary Player, won seven Masters in a row between 1960 and 1966.

CBS televised the tournament for the first in 1956. In an effort to boost ticket sales, the broadcast was blacked out within a 200-mile radius of Augusta.

Fortunately, for CBS and for Augusta National, the dawn of the TV era coincided with the arrival of people-pleasing Arnold Palmer.

The Masters, like the World Series, the Indianapolis 500 and the Kentucky Derby, suddenly became a must-see event—even for those viewers who didn't otherwise particularly care about golf.

The first Masters telecast, snowy and black-and-white, nevertheless attracted an estimated 10 million viewers coast to coast.

Golfers gathered in grill rooms across the country to catch a glimpse of the glorious course that they, until then, had only heard about.

When some of the Masters participants complained about the TV equipment and personnel on the course, Clifford Roberts prophetically pointed out that, if the telecasts caught on, they could elevate the Masters and the game beyond anyone's wildest dreams.

Masters officials have always been very protective of their tournament's image.

In 1966, often-eloquent television commentator Jack Whitaker made the mistake of referring to the throng that was running up Augusta's 18th fairway in order to get a better view of the green during Monday's three-way playoff featuring Jack Nicklaus, as a "mob."

Masters officials were not pleased. Patrons, after all, could not possibly constitute a mob.

As a result, Whitaker was not a part of CBS's Masters coverage for the next six years. And he never again was the lead announcer at Augusta.

In 1994, golfer/announcer Gary McCord, trying as usual to be amusing and entertaining, mentioned "body bags" and "bikini wax" in the midst of the widely watched Sunday afternoon Masters telecast.

As a result, he, too, was promptly removed from the Masters broadcast team.

As McCord later described his double faux pas:

When Jose Maria Olazabal reached the 17th hole and began conferring with his caddie in Spanish,

Billy Casper

McCord informed the TV audience that he would interpret their conversation.

"Olazabal is telling his caddie that the only thing he doesn't want to do is hit it over the green," McCord announced. "It's DOA down there."

Contrary to McCord's warning, Olazabal lofted his shot over the green and the ball began rolling down the embankment. McCord reported that if the ball rolled any farther, they would need some "body bags" because Olazabal would be "dead down there."

That was Mistake No. 1.

Minutes later, Tom Lehman, trailing by two strokes, found himself on the green, facing a critical putt. In an attempt to convey to his listeners how fast the greens at Augusta are, McCord quipped that they were coated with "bikini wax."

Exit McCord. He has not been heard at stately Augusta since.

Doug Sanders, still one of the game's snappiest dressers, showed up at the 1965 Masters wearing bright yellow slacks, shirt and shoes.

"I hear we're on color TV today," Sanders explained.

Colorful Lee Trevino has won 56 tournaments on the PGA and Senior Tours. But he has never come close to winning at Augusta National. He has long maintained the golf course doesn't suit the low, left-to-right flight of his ball.

In addition, the eighth-grade dropout who grew up in a shack alongside an East Dallas golf course, never felt completely comfortable in Augusta's somewhat pretentious environment.

Trevino declined invitations to the 1970 and 1971 Masters even though he was one of the leading players in the world at the time. When he returned in 1972—at the urging of Jack Nicklaus and others—Trevino became embroiled in a dispute when officials sought to remove Lee's chauffeur from the grounds, claiming he didn't have the proper credential.

Trevino threatened to leave, too, and later refused to use the clubhouse. Instead, he changed his shoes in the players' parking lot.

Trevino insisted he fled the clubhouse because it was full of reporters. "Had nothing to do with Augusta," he said.

One year, as Trevino was preparing to depart after a practice round, Chi Chi Rodriguez shouted at him from the nearby bleachers.

"Hey, they don't allow Mexicans in here!" Rodriguez yelled, with a grin on his face.

"Okay," Trevino replied, laughing. "I'm leaving."

Six-foot-six George Archer only took up golf because he had been kicked off his junior high school basketball team for skipping practice.

"I never thought about winning the Masters," Archer admitted after his one-stroke victory over Billy Casper, Tom Weiskopf and George Knudson, earned him a green jacket in 1969—the only major championship of his career. "That's like aiming at the moon."

Later, Archer regaled reporters with tales of his lack of prowess, while growing up on a ranch.

"What I did on the ranch was clean out the stalls and water troughs and paint fences," Archer explained. "Certain fellows used to ride horses on the ranch but I never got to be as high class as a cowboy."

Billy Casper, father of 11 children and winner of three majors, was heartbroken when he shot a 40 on the front side of the final round of the 1969 Masters and eventually fell to Archer by one shot.

But the 38-year-old Casper atoned the following April when he easily ousted long-time friend Gene Littler by five shots in their 1970 Masters playoff.

As the two men teed it up for the Monday show-down, Casper turned to Littler and said, "It took us 72 holes to get rid of those other guys."

Tied with Sam Snead for the tournament lead on the final day of the 1957 Masters, Doug Ford and his caddie got into a dispute on the 15th hole.

Ford wanted to play it safe and lay up, but his caddie insisted he should go for the green.

Stuffing his 4-iron back in his bag, Ford pulled out his 3-wood and said, "Here goes the whole ballgame."

His caddie was right. Ford's shot landed on the green, leaving him an easy birdie and an eventual four-stroke victory over Sam Snead.

"They don't remember if you finish second here," Ford remarked afterward.

Ford described himself as "a gorilla golfer.

"I'm not pretty to look at our there," Ford admitted. "My swing is far from a picture swing. I have to fight the ball and fight the course all the way around, sort of the way a gorilla would go at it."

Lew Worsham's tee shot on the 12th hole in 1951, landed in the water, then bounced out of the pond and up onto the green, from where Worsham was able to record one of the most remarkable birdies, not only in Masters, but in major tournament history.

When hot-tempered Tommy Bolt made a double bogey 6 on No. 18 to finish with a disappointing 74 in the second round in 1956, he knew who to blame.

"I hit a bad shot out of the sand trap, and some so-and-so yelled, 'Break it! Go ahead and break the club,'" Bolt bristled.

"It was one of those idiots who is too lazy to go out on the course. What kind of game is this, when a guy yells like he's at a baseball game?"

Never a winner at Augusta National, Tom Weiskopf finished second four times, tying Ben Hogan and Jack Nicklaus for that dubious distinction.

Of course, Hogan and Nicklaus also won eight Masters between them.

Amateur sensation Ken Venturi appeared a certain victor in 1956 when his closest challenger, Cary Middlecoff, who was four strokes back, made three double-bogeys.

But baby-faced former Marine Jackie Burke Jr. fired a final-round 71 to make up an eight-shot deficit and grab the green jacket in the first Masters broadcast on national TV.

"I was running away from Cary Middlecoff," explained Venturi, who finished with an 80, "and the door hit me on the way out."

Painstakingly slow and meticulous on the golf course, Cary Middlecoff, who had been an outstanding amateur player, nevertheless waited until he had completed his training as a dentist before turning pro.

Middlecoff wanted to have something to fall back on, in case he failed on the links.

"The Doc" finished second by a then-record five shots behind club pro Claude Harmon in the 1948 Masters, but defeated Ben Hogan by a record seven strokes at Augusta in 1955.

Ed Furgol accidentally struck a woman in the face when his ball sailed over the 15th green in 1963.

The woman was rushed to the hospital but suffered no broken bones.

"I never have had much luck with women," admitted Furgol, who bogeyed the hole.

In 1954, while stationed at nearby Fort Gordon, 1967 Masters champion Gay Brewer parked cars at Augusta National. That was the year Sam Snead beat Ben Hogan, 70 to 71, in just the third playoff in Masters history.

In 1966, Brewer needed only to par the final hole at Augusta to claim his first major championship.

Instead, he bogeyed the hole, forcing a three-way playoff with Jack Nicklaus and Tommy Jacobs, where Brewer shot a disappointing 78 to finish third.

The following year, however, Brewer bounced back with a vengeance at Augusta, beating Bobby Nichols by a single stroke to earn the green jacket.

Brewer attended the University of Kentucky on a football scholarship. His position was holding the ball in place for the field goal kickers—in practice, but never during the actual games.

Brewer's biggest worry was that one of the kickers would miss the football and kick his hand, impeding his touch on the golf course.

At the 1950 Masters, runner-up Jim Ferrier's wife, Norma, ducked under the ropes after every one of her husband's tee shots and walked with him to his ball on every hole.

Then she would go back under the ropes and re-join Ferrier after he had finished putting.

Needing only to shoot a 38 on the back nine on the final round to win the 1950 tournament, Ferrier—who placed second behind Sam Snead on the PGA Tour money list that season—could do no better than 41, good for second place behind Jimmy Demaret.

Bert Yancey was so obsessed with winning the Masters that he built clay models of each of Augusta National's 18 greens to study and peruse during the tournament.

They didn't help much. Although Yancey led after two rounds in 1967, and finished fourth or better three times in four years, he never achieved the victory he coveted above all others.

When Charles Coody won the 1971 Masters, he dined all week on sweet potato biscuits, wore his lucky, light green trousers, and marked his ball with an English half-penny that his eight-year-old daughter had given him.

Former playboy Raymond Floyd rocked Augusta in 1976 when he shot 271 to win the tournament and match Jack Nicklaus' 11-year-old scoring record.

Bobby Jones labeled dentist Cary Middlecoff's 65 on the second round of the 1955 Masters, "The greatest round in the history of the tournament."

"This is a waiting kind of golf course," Middlecoff explained. "If you shoot for birds, you'll bogey every hole."

As if to prove his point, Middlecoff made twice as many birdies (18) as bogeys (9) that year.

Using a new mallet-headed putter, bespectacled Art Wall Jr. upstaged fan favorite and defending champion Arnold Palmer to win the 1959 Masters.

Prior to the final round, Wall was packing his car for the trip home when Gene Sarazen, who like most of the golfers was staying in the downtown Bon Air Hotel, walked by.

"Go out and have a good finish," Sarazen urged.

Little did either man know.

Later, talking to a reporter in the locker room, Wall mentioned that a final round 66 "might give somebody a scare.

"I was just talking through my hat," Wall admitted.

Nevertheless, Wall birdied five of the final six holes to shoot—you guessed it, a 66—to edge Cary Middlecoff by one stroke in one of the greatest finishes in Masters history.

"A guy like me gets only one or two chances in a lifetime to win a major," Wall admitted years later. And Wall certainly made the most of his.

7

Bobby

"Golf without (Bob) Jones would be like France without Paris."

— *sportswriter Herbert Warren Wind*

Only baseball's legendary Babe Ruth overshadowed dashing, daring, young Bobby Jones during sports' "Golden Age," which also included Jack Dempsey, Red Grange and Bill Tilden.

At his peak, Jones was almost indomitable on the golf course, winning 13 of the 21 major championships he entered from 1923 through 1930.

During the decade of 1920s, Jones entered 45 tournaments, won 21 of them and finished second seven times.

In September, 1930, Jones, who never turned pro, won the U.S. Amateur at Philadelphia's Merion Golf

Club—completing an unprecedented clean sweep of all four of what were then considered golf's major championships: The U.S. and British Opens and the U.S. and British Amateurs.

No golfer had ever won all four of golf's biggest tournaments in the same year. And none have done it since, although Tiger Woods did achieve an asterisked modern era Grand Slam when he swept the 2000 U.S. and British Opens and PGA Championship, followed by the 2001 Masters.

When Gene Homans, Jones' unheralded opponent that historic 1930 September afternoon, missed an 18-foot putt on the 11th hole, he immediately extended his hand in congratulation. Jones had won the match, and the U.S. Amateur championship, 8 and 7.

Years later, Jones recalled, "All at once I felt the wonderful feeling of release from tension and relaxation that I had wanted so badly for so long a time."

At age 28, Jones had done it all.

Little did anyone suspect at the time that except for his annual Masters appearance, Bobby Jones—Bob to his friends—had played his last competitive round. Two months later, the game's greatest player retired as an active competitor.

Jones was tired of the pressure of competition. It was time to pursue his other dream.

Jones' well-heeled friends and supporters would regularly wager huge sums of money on their hero, whenever and wherever he played. When Jones failed to come through in the clutch, as he inevitably did on occasion, he invariably felt as if he had let his buddies down.

At the time, Augusta was a small, quaint, Old South winter golf haven for the wealthy. With the financial support of some of those same affluent friends, Jones purchased the abandoned 365-acre Fruitlands Nursery in Augusta for $75,000 at the height of the Great Depression and built the golf course retreat of his dreams—a place where he and his pals could laugh, drink, and play golf in privacy.

Reluctantly, Jones would come out of retirement each year to play in the tournament he had created at Augusta National.

Clifford Roberts wrote: "Bobby Jones has agreed to make this tournament the one exception to his rule against further participation in tournament golf. He does this with the thought of helping to establish a new golfing event that is hoped may assume the proportion of an important tournament."

Jones' friend and Augusta National member Grantland Rice, who also happened to be honorary chairman of the first Masters, shamelessly heralded Bobby's return in his nationally syndicated newspaper column.

But the effects of Jones' long absence from serious competition were obvious.

Jones shot 76-74-72-72 and finished in a tie for 13th place, 10 strokes behind Horton Smith, in the inaugural 1934 Masters.

Jones abhorred the idea of turning professional. He once described the typical club pro as "an uneducated club servant."

In those days, professionals were often barred from even setting foot in the more snooty clubhouses around the country.

Jones was the ultimate amateur. But, under USGA rules, in 1934 Jones could technically no longer be considered an amateur.

He had been paid to make a series of instructional golf films for Warner Bros. and he had been hired by A.G. Spalding & Bros. to design and promote his own line of golf clubs.

At the time of the first Masters, Jones was earning more than $100,000 a year from golf-related endeavors—a princely sum in those Depression days.

Bobby Jones

By comparison, Paul Runyan, the PGA Tour's leading money winner in 1934, made just $6,767.

Although he never was a real factor in any of the 12 Masters in which he played, Jones remained a sentimental favorite of the fans.

In 1948, Jones shot 76-81-79-79 and never played in the Masters again.

Club members chipped in to buy the ailing Jones a golf cart so he could get out on the course to watch the tournament.

Jones attended his final Masters in 1968 and died in December, 1971.

"Everybody adored him," wrote famed golf writer Herbert Warren Wind. "Not just dyed-in-the-wool golfers, but people who had never struck a ball or had the least desire to. He was the model American athlete come to life.

"They admired the ingrained modesty, the humor, the generosity of spirit that were evident in Jones' remarks and deportment. They liked the way he looked, this handsome, clean-cut young man, whose eyes gleamed with both a frank boyishness and a perceptiveness far beyond his years."

The similarities between Bobby Jones and Tiger Woods are many.

Jones hit his first golf shot when he was five. By age nine, Jones was playing against grown men and winning the junior championship at East Lake Golf Club in Atlanta, defeating a boy seven years older.

By the time he was 12, Jones was shooting 70. He was not yet wearing long trousers. At 13, he won the East Lake club championship, as well as the title at nearby Druid Hills. The next year he won the Georgia Amateur. At 21, he was the U.S. Open champion.

From 1923-30, Jones won five U.S. Amateurs, four U.S. Opens, three British Opens, and one British Amateur—13 of the 21 major tournaments in which he competed during that incredible eight-year span.

As a youngster, Woods suffered from a speech impediment that caused him to stutter. Jones was frail and gaunt as a child and had a serious digestive disorder that until he was five, threatened his life.

Later, Jones was crippled by syringomelia, a debilitating disease of the spinal cord that causes the body to waste away.

Much of the public assumed he merely suffered from arthritis. "Just let it go at that," Jones said. "It (arthritis) is easier to understand."

Cool and calculating on the outside, Jones was often a nervous wreck inside. He couldn't eat during major tournaments. Dry toast and tea were all that his stomach would tolerate.

At times, without apparent provocation, Jones would suddenly double over in pain, vomiting and even bursting into tears due to the intense pressure he felt because of the public's expectations.

"Why should I punish myself like this over a golf tournament?" he once asked.

Like Tiger Woods, Robert Tyre Jones Jr. could have cashed in on his performance and popularity and made a fortune.

Unlike Tiger, Jones turned down millions in endorsements after he retired from tournament play. Ever the amateur, he abhorred the commercial side of sports.

However, in addition to his duties as a practicing attorney, Jones helped develop his own line of golf clubs for Spalding, and made a series of 16 short instructional movie features for Warner Brothers. He also owned a couple of profitable Coca-Cola bottling franchises.

At the annual Masters Past Champions Dinner, players frequently voice their opinions on the current conditions and demands of the golf course.

One year, several champions complained about the severity of one green in particular.

Finally Bobby Jones, who attended every dinner until his death in 1971, had heard enough.

"You boys make me sick," the Masters founder said. "You think it's your right to birdie every hole. I recall that when I was playing, par was still a pretty good score."

Bobby Jones' father, Robert P. Jones, also affectionately known as "The Colonel," was good enough as a baseball player to be offered a contract with the Brooklyn Dodgers.

But The Colonel's father, Robert Tyre Jones Sr.—Bobby Jones' grandfather—quickly squashed that idea. "I didn't send you to college to become a professional baseball player," Bobby Jones' grandfather told the future golfing great's dad.

In addition to being a successful industrialist, Robert T. Jones Sr. was also the founder and a deacon of the Canton (Georgia) First Baptist Church.

"Bob, if you must play on Sunday," the elder Jones told his world-famous grandson, "play well."

Gene Sarazen, who won the second Masters in 1935, first became Jones' friend in 1920. The two men frequently played practice rounds together and were occasionally paired in the early tournaments.

The two men had a standing bet: The first one to throw a club owed the other $10, a sizable sum in those days.

In his younger days, Jones was notorious for throwing clubs after bad shots. At the age of 14, he competed in the U.S. Amateur and upset Eben Byers, another golfer infamous for his bad temper and club tossing. Years later Jones liked to joke that he only won that match because Byers ran out of clubs before he did.

However, Jones conquered his temper almost as quickly as he mastered the game.

"There wasn't much talking," Sarazen recalled years later, "because every time he played a shot, the gallery would start to run. He was the Tiger Woods of his time."

8

The Amateurs

"I jumped up and down for an hour or so. It was just unbelievable."

> — *Australian amateur Aaron Baddeley, upon receiving his invitation to the 2000 Masters*

Masters founder Bobby Jones was the consummate amateur.

That is why the Masters—much more so than the U.S. or British Opens—pampers the amateurs it invites to participate each April.

They are feted with a special dinner and housed for the week in the historic "Crows' Nest" in the clubhouse, where they are allowed to sign for their meals.

Jack Nicklaus made his Masters debut as an amateur of 1959. It was an experience he will never forget.

"I had obtained permission to spend time well ahead of the Masters practicing at Augusta National," Nicklaus recalled. "To protect our amateur status, I suppose, we were charged only a nominal rate for meals—as I recall, a dollar for breakfast, a dollar for lunch, and two dollars for dinner.

"The only person I know who enjoys eating more than I do is Phil Rodgers. And he had also decided to get in some early work on site that year as an amateur invitee.

"Immediately after golf, Phil and I would hasten to the dining room, where we would begin with a double shrimp cocktail, then each polish off a couple of sirloin steaks with all the trimmings. If we felt like it, we would go on to a third steak.

"After four days, they clamped down on Phil and me," Nicklaus continued. "They wouldn't let us order two steaks apiece anymore. But we were still allowed a shrimp cocktail."

During the first two rounds each April, the amateurs are paired with some of Augusta's greatest former champions.

"You're thinking, 'I can't believe this,'" recalled 1991 U.S. Amateur champion Mitch Voges, who played in the '92 Masters. "You're part of the history of the game."

No golf tournament is more clothes-conscious than the Masters. But nobody said a word in 2001 when 23-year-old amateur James Driscoll showed up wearing seersucker trousers, a lilac shirt and a red baseball cap.

"I'm not really a consistent dresser," Driscoll explained.

Los Angeles caddie and amateur invitee Greg Puga's faux pas was even more embarrassing.

"On Wednesday, I was walking to the range before my practice round and signing autographs," the 30-year-old Puga confessed. "I approached Arnold Palmer and he was looking at me with his hands on his hips. He looked kinda mad.

"He said to me, 'You need to fix that.' He was pointing down. I looked down and my fly was open."

In 1954, amateur Ken Venturi, playing in his first Masters, found himself paired with the great Ben Hogan.

After the usual pleasantries, Hogan informed Venturi that he could stop calling him "Mr. Hogan," and call him "Ben" instead.

On the par-3 4th hole, Hogan watched Venturi hit a 3-iron onto the green.

That was enough to convince Hogan to hit a 3-iron of his own. However, Hogan's ball ended up in a bunker.

At which point, Venturi said, "I guess that means you want me to call you 'Mr. Hogan.'"

Ken Venturi finished second as an amateur in 1956. Had he won, Venturi planned to remain an amateur and not play professionally.

He had been promised a vice-presidency with Ford Motor Company and reasoned he would make more money doing that than he could on the PGA Tour.

When he squandered a four-stroke lead with an 80 on Sunday and fell short at Augusta, Venturi felt he had to prove himself by turning pro.

Matt Kuchar, an apple-cheeked college kid with a toothy smile, stole the show at the 1998 Masters with his eagerness, his exuberance and his optimism.

Ben Crenshaw

Few players ever caused such a fuss in their Masters debut. And few ever had as much fun.

"Cornbread!" Kuchar would exclaim. Or "Cheese and crackers!" The sacred course has never heard such language.

When Kuchar made a good shot, of which he made many en route to a 21st place finish—the best by an amateur in 16 years—he would turn to his gallery, that grew by the day, and grin in wide-eyed wonder. When he struck the ball poorly, which he occasionally did, he would flash a sheepish smile.

"Matt's performance in 1998 was magnificent," raved green-jacketed Charlie Yates, the lone surviving amateur from the inaugural Masters in 1934, a 12-time participant and a member at Augusta National.

"Not only in the way he played," added Yates, who was a close friend of Bobby Jones, "but in the way he handled himself."

On Sunday evening, Kuchar and his caddie/father Peter were invited to the club members' annual dinner honoring the new champion, Mark O'Meara.

O'Meara, of course, received a standing ovation from the green-jacketed elite. And Kuchar did, too.

After dinner, Kuchar and his dad headed for the Crows' Nest—the cramped dormitory on the third floor of the historic clubhouse, where amateurs traditionally stay during the tournament—to retrieve Matt's belongings.

As they came down the aged stairs, they paused outside the fabled Champions' Locker Room, as Tiger Woods and so many other amateurs have done before them.

"We stayed there a moment," Peter Kuchar explained, "just to soak up the feeling and the history of the room."

"All of Augusta has an aura about it," Matt added. "But the Champions' Locker Room is special place."

Nineteen-year-old college freshman Tiger Woods shot 72-72-77-72 as an amateur in his Augusta National debut in 1995.

In the early years, several amateurs such as Frank Stanahan, Billy Joe Patton, Ken Venturi and Charlie Coe actually challenged the professionals for the Masters championship.

One year, pro Lloyd Mangrum informed Coe: "I don't care very much to play with an amateur."

To which Coe responded: "I don't care very much to play with a pro."

As the 1968 U.S. Amateur champion, Bruce Fleisher earned an invitation to the '69 Masters.

Young Fleisher showed up for his first practice round at Augusta National wearing bell-bottom trousers that were considered quite hip in those days.

Masters chairman Clifford Roberts ordered him never to set foot on the golf course in those pants again.

Since bell bottoms were all that Fleisher had brought with him, he went out that evening and bought himself a new wardrobe.

Ben Crenshaw's U.S. Amateur championship earned him an invitation to the 1972 Masters.

As the 21-year-old Crenshaw left the scorer's tent after an opening-round 73, he encountered tournament chairman Clifford Roberts.

"How did you enjoy your first round in the Masters, Ben?" Roberts inquired.

"Very much, Mr. Roberts," Crenshaw respectfully replied.

"That's fine, Ben," Roberts said. "And I think you'll enjoy it a lot more if you go get a haircut."

On what old-timers still remember as one of the windiest days in Masters history, amateur George Kunkle shot a humbling 95 on the fourth and final round of the 1956 tournament, including a 49 on the front side.

Wealthy Frank Stranahan, who tied for second in 1947, matching Ken Venturi (1956) and Charlie Coe (1961) for the best finish ever by an amateur, was kicked off the course and out of the tournament in 1948 after Stranahan become involved in a squabble with an Augusta National employee.

Players are only permitted to play one ball during practice rounds, but Stranahan had repeatedly broken that rule prior to the 1947 tournament and gotten away with it.

As a result, early in Stranahan's first practice round in 1948, course superintendent Marion Luke approached him on the course twice to remind him of the rule.

Stranahan later insisted all he had done was drop several extra balls to practice his putting.

Angry words were exchanged, and Luke reported the incident to Roberts. Several Augusta National members were waiting for Stranahan when he arrived at the eighth green.

"We're taking away your permission to play," one of the members informed him. "Your invitation has been withdrawn. Please leave the golf course."

Stranahan, who finished second in the 1947 Masters, had to buy a ticket to watch the tournament in 1948.

Eventually, Stranahan was invited to play in 11 more Masters, but his best finishes were ties for 14th in 1950 and 1953.

Even as a amateur, Stranahan, heir to the Champion Spark Plug fortune, spent as many 45 weeks a year on the road, playing golf.

To help him cope with that rigorous lifestyle, Stranahan, an avid body builder, traveled with 365 pounds of barbells and weights.

Watching aging or undersized hotel bellboys and porters struggle to carry his luggage to and from the trunk of his Cadillac convertible was quite a sight.

British Amateur champion Graeme Storm brought his mother to caddy for him in 2000—a Masters first.

Jane Storm tried on three of the white jumpsuits that caddies traditionally wear at Augusta National before trimming six inches off the legs and arms of a set of coveralls to make them fit.

Seven years after Australian Aaron Baddeley first picked up a golf club, he was playing Augusta National in the 2000 Masters.

It was Baddeley's grandmother who got him started. His father and mother didn't even play. Baddeley was 12 years old at the time.

Eleven months later, Baddeley had lowered his handicap from 23 to 6. Jack Nicklaus himself wrote the youngster a letter. "I don't know how he got my name, address or anything," Baddeley said.

At age 14, he won his club championship. It was then that Aaron turned to his dad and said, "I don't care what I do in life, but it's going to have something to do with golf."

When he graduated from high school in Australia, 25 U.S. colleges offered Baddeley scholarships. "He hits the ball better than I did at his age," admitted Tiger Woods, who knows a little something about young phenoms.

"This is what I've dreamed of, ever since I started playing," admitted the American-born Australian Open champion, who was 19 when he made his Augusta debut.

"As you drive up Magnolia Lane, you see the trees overhanging, and you see the flowers, and you're thinking, 'I'm at Augusta.' Knowing a 19-year-old is driving up at Augusta is such a good feeling. I know a lot of friends back home would like to be in the same position. You watch it on the telly, you think of all the guys that have played here, Hogan, Snead, Sarazen, it's great. I love the Masters.

"I've dreamed of it so vividly," he added, "it's not out of reality that I'm here."

According to his father, Ron Baddeley—who was working as the chief mechanic on Mario Andretti's Indy car racing team and living in New Hampshire when Aaron was born—once the youngster picked up a golf club, he refused to put it down.

"I used to have to take it away from him," Ron Baddeley recalled. "I had to make rules, like no putting on the carpet. It was seven days a week. He was so intense."

Since then, Baddeley has become a protégé of fellow-Australian Greg Norman.

"When I was his age, I was probably still on a surf board," quipped Norman. "I haven't taken him under my wing, so to speak. The thing I've done is let him sit down and ask me questions. About anything. I feel very attached to him.

"I was like that when I was a kid. I never had any problem going up to Jack Nicklaus or going up to Arnold Palmer and asking for advice.

"The thing I like about Aaron is the fact he believes in himself," Norman continued. "I like the fact that he's very eager. I also like the fact that he's very humble.

"On top of that, he's got a good game. A game that's only going to get better and better. All he wants to do is hit balls, practice and play, hit balls, practice and play.

"The thing I told him was, 'Decide where you want to be 20 years from now,'" Norman added. "In 20 years, he's still only going to be 39. He's still a puppy."

Baddeley was the first Australian amateur to play in the Masters, but not the first to receive an invitation.

House painter Harry Berwick was invited in 1957 but couldn't afford to make the trip.

Long-driving North Carolina lumber executive Billy Joe Patton prepped for the 1954 Masters by hitting golf balls during his lunch breaks.

Before he departed for Augusta, Patton purchased a new white sport coat. "For the trophy presentation," he explained.

Patton never lacked for confidence.

Five strokes behind Ben Hogan, and two behind Sam Snead when play began on Sunday in 1954, the bespectacled Patton jumped back into contention with a hole-in-one on the sixth hole.

Over the years, the 180-yard No. 6 had earned a reputation as the fifth-toughest hole on the golf course. It had never been aced in the Masters until 1954, when both Leland Gibson and Patton recorded holes-in-one.

Patton proceeded to birdie the eighth and ninth holes, catching Hogan and passing Snead. The amateur was on his way.

But Patton's aggressive nature got him into trouble on the back nine and he eventually ended one stroke behind both Hogan and Snead.

"I didn't come to play safe," Patton said.

"Nobody called me reckless when I made the hole-in-one."

9

By Invitation Only

"Drinks were on the house for everyone at the first tournament. I remember they had 150 gallons of white lightning in the clubhouse. And by the morning of the third day, they ran out."

— *Paul Runyan*

When Augusta National first opened in 1933, during the Great Depression, the club boasted a mere 59 members, even though it cost only $350 to join.

Eager for national recognition, Bobby Jones and Clifford Roberts offered to host the 1934 U.S. Open at Augusta National.

Jones, knowing that the summer heat in Augusta can be brutal, insisted that the tournament be played in March or April. But the USGA didn't want to depart from its traditional June dates and declined the invitation.

That was when Jones and Roberts decided to host a tournament of their own.

The Masters was originally known as "Augusta National Invitation Tournament." And at the magnificent, majestic, mythical Masters, an "invitation" still means everything.

Although the tournament now bases its guest list partially on the Official World Golf Rankings, the game's greatest players still must be "invited" to participate in the annual Masters.

They play at the pleasure of the rich and powerful gentlemen in green jackets. Playing Augusta National is a privilege as well as a pleasure.

Today, all golfers crave an invitation to play in the Masters and PGA Tour regulars often complain when, for one reason or another, they don't get one.

But that wasn't always the case.

Miami Beach club pro Willie Klein declined an invitation to play in the first Masters because he was "too busy."

Former PGA and U.S. Open champion Olin Dutra gave a similar excuse. "My duties at my home club compel me to remain at home," he wrote.

The field for the inaugural Masters was set strictly on an invitational basis. However, by 1935, Bobby Jones and Clifford Roberts had drawn up a basic list of automatic qualifiers.

They included:

1. Past and present U.S. Open champions
2. Past and present U.S. Amateur champions
3. Past and present British Open champions
4. Past and present British Amateur champions
5. Current members of the Walker Cup team
6. Current members of the U.S. Ryder Cup team
7. The top 24 finishers from the previous year's Augusta National Invitation Tournament

In 1974, Lee Elder defeated Peter Oosterhuis in a playoff to win the Monsanto Open in Pensacola, Florida, and thus, in '75, became the first black golfer to participate in the Masters.

In the Augusta galleries, spectators wore buttons that read, "Good Luck, Lee."

"It was a very nervous time for me," admitted Elder on the 25th anniversary of his historic breakthrough. "I had never been involved in anything like that."

Although Elder missed the cut in 1975, he participated in five of the next six Masters. His best effort occurred in 1979 when he finished 17th.

In 1947, Freddie Haas, who as an amateur had been personally invited to play in the 1936 Masters by Bobby Jones himself, was lining up a putt on the third round of the tournament when a golfer in the group behind him hit his ball onto the green.

After Haas had finished putting and teed off on the ninth hole, he returned to the eighth green to confront Johnny Bulla, whom he had identified as the guilty party.

"Hey, you hit into me," Haas informed Bulla. "Somebody could have gotten hurt."

That was all he said.

After Haas finished his round, tournament chairman Clifford Roberts summoned him to his clubhouse office.

"Fred," Roberts said, "we don't tolerate than kind of attitude around here. If you will write a letter of apology, we might have you back again."

Haas, who in reality had doing nothing wrong other than raise his voice, wrote the letter, and Roberts invited him back.

In 1989, Bernhard Langer, who had arrived at Augusta National a week early in order to prepare for the tournament, was playing several balls at one time and putting from various places on the greens during a practice round.

That apparently perturbed the Augusta National members who were playing a leisurely round behind him.

When Langer returned to the clubhouse, club chairman Hord Hardin unceremoniously informed him that being a former Masters winner did not necessarily guarantee him future invitations to play in the event.

Horton Smith's second-round eagle on the 17th hole (now No. 8), and a clutch 20-foot putt two days

Bernhard Langer

later on the final round contributed to his one-stroke victory over Craig Wood in the inaugural Masters in 1934.

Smith received a check for $1,500—which exceeded the top prize money at any of the other three major championships, including the U.S. Open, that year.

Tournament chairman Clifford Roberts passed the hat among the Augusta National's founding members to raise the $5,000 purse, making the record payoff possible.

The club collected only $8,011 in ticket sales at the first tournament, which was not even enough to cover the costs of preparing the course and pay the employees.

However, the inaugural Masters was successful enough to entice 18 or 20 new members to join the club, pumping more than $6,000 in initiation fees into the empty Augusta National coffers.

In 1936, in a tournament marred by fog and nine inches of rain, Horton Smith holed out a 50-foot chip shot on his way to his second Masters title.

The two Masters were the only majors Smith ever won.

In 1963, the Masters broke one of its many rules and allowed an aging Smith, by then in failing health, to ride an electric cart during his final round. Smith shot 42 on the front side, before finishing with a 92.

Tickets to the first Masters—good for all four days of the tournament, plus the preceding four days of practice—cost $5, plus 50 cents tax.

Tickets to the Masters didn't sell out for the first time until 1966. At that time, a ticket for Saturday or Sunday's rounds sold for $7.50.

Liquor flowed freely at Augusta National in the early years.

"Drinks were on the house for everyone at the first tournament," recalled diminutive Paul Runyan, affectionately known as "Little Poison," who participated in the first 13 Masters and led the PGA Tour in victories in 1933 and 1934, despite being unable to drive the ball much farther than 200 yards.

"I remember they had 150 gallons of white lightning in the clubhouse. And by the morning of the third day, they ran out. Yes, they got some more."

At the inaugural Masters tournament, the participants were quartered at the Bon Air Vanderbilt hotel in downtown Augusta at a rate of $5 per player per night. And that special price included three meals a day.

Today during the Masters the cheapest motel rooms in town rent for at least $200 a night and many of the nicer places charge twice that amount.

And nearly every room in the area is booked months in advance.

Soon after the classic 1942 Byron Nelson versus Ben Hogan showdown, Augusta National was shut down for the duration of World War II.

Neighbors took advantage of the closure to ride motor bikes over Augusta National's hilly terrain. Kids frequently went swimming in Rae's Creek.

Members were each assessed $100 a year in maintenance fees, and 200 head of Hereford steers and a flock of turkeys were allowed to graze on the golf course until the Masters returned 1946.

Jones and Roberts assumed that the cattle would help keep the Bermuda grass on the course in check and could eventually be sold to defray expenses.

In fact, the club lost $5,000 on the cattle, not counting the damage the animals did to Augusta National's flowers and shrubs.

But the club made money on the turkeys—some of which were killed and shipped to Augusta National members for Christmas dinner.

To prepare for the resumption of play in 1946, Roberts "borrowed" 42 German prisoners of war from nearby Fort Gordon to manicure the neglected grounds back to Masters' standards.

For six months, the POWs, who had been part of Rommel's famed Africa Korps, were picked up at Fort Gordon each morning and returned at night.

When the Masters resumed in 1946, the unlikely winner was lanky Herman Keiser, who had served as a storekeeper on the cruiser USS Cincinnati during World War II and spent his final summer of military service fine-tuning his swing at a driving range near Norfolk, Virginia, where he was based.

Betting on the Masters—by players, as well as by Augusta National patrons—was commonplace in the early years, and the fun-loving Keiser, who oddly enough was known as "the Missouri Mortician" because of his gloomy demeanor, wagered $20 on himself to win.

Ben Hogan was far and away the betting favorite, and after Keiser stunned the field by firing 69-68 on the first two rounds to lead Hogan by seven strokes, the surprise tournament leader began to suspect that people were conspiring against him.

As Keiser, who once worked as an assistant under inaugural Masters winner Horton Smith, confidently walked off the course after the second round, a bookmaker quietly informed him that a couple of influential Augusta National members had wagered $50,000 apiece on Hogan to win.

That was a tremendous sum of money in those days, and when tournament officials refused to allow Keiser to replace his limping, sore-footed caddie, the normally pessimistic golfer perceived that as part of a plot to see to it that he didn't win.

When Keiser, who was eating lunch, nearly missed his tee time for the third-round—which Herman claimed had been changed without notifying him—he became even more paranoid.

When legendary sportswriter and founding Augusta National member Grantland Rice came out on the course to threaten Keiser with a penalty if he didn't speed up the pace of his play, Keiser was certain something was amiss.

"Someone didn't want me to win," he said.

Somehow, in spite of his paranoia, Keiser hung on to defeat the great Hogan by one shot after both men three-putted the final hole of the tournament.

Outgoing Jimmy Demaret won three Masters (1940, 1947, and 1950). But you will find no monuments at Augusta National named after him.

"I can't even get an outhouse named for me," joked Demaret, whose off-the-cuff comments once earned him a written reprimand from Bobby Jones.

"Golf and sex," Demaret was fond of saying, "are the only things you can enjoy without being good at them."

Playing in an era when it was not at all unusual to see golfers on the course in neckties, Demaret favored garish outfits—the louder and more outlandish the better—and an oversized tam.

For Demaret, green suede shoes, chartreuse trousers, red belts, yellow socks, and pink sweaters were the norm.

"If you're going to be in the limelight, you might as well dress like it," Demaret explained.

Demaret blamed his love of gaudy colors on his father, a housepainter, who had occasionally allowed little Jimmy to mix his paint.

Jimmy Demaret

"He was the life spirit of our tour," recalled fellow PGA Tour pioneer Paul Runyan. "He was everybody's friend and extremely popular with his peers."

After winning his first Masters in 1940, Demaret had to rush back to Houston where he was the head pro at Brae Burn Country Club. "I was scared somebody might steal my job," he explained.

In 1947, Demaret used 16 birdies to become the first player to post four sub-par rounds in the same Masters.

Demaret—finished for the day and tied with Jim Ferrier, who was still out on the course, for the 1950 tournament lead after four rounds—was relaxing in the radio tower alongside the 18th green and pondering the possibility of a playoff the next day.

"If he ties me, I'll beat him tomorrow," Demaret vowed.

But Ferrier bogeyed five of the last six holes including the final two to give Jimmy his third Masters title.

When Bobby Jones presented Demaret with the winner's check for $2,400 at the ceremonies afterwards, the irrepressible Demaret, a former nightclub singer, grabbed the microphone and began to sing, "How Lucky You Are."

No one ever accused Demaret of being politically correct.

At the start of the Masters one year he approached Argentinian Robert De Vicenzo, who would later become infamous for his 1968 scoring blunder, and informed him: "Roberto, play as good as you can. I'm betting on you to be low Mexican."

Club Professional Claude Harmon was on his way home to Winged Foot in New York from his winter job in Florida in 1948 when he stopped off at Augusta.

He definitely made it worth his while, defying the odds by outdistancing runner-up Cary Middlecoff by what was then a record five strokes to win the Masters.

It was, by the way, the first and only tournament win of Harmon's otherwise undistinguished professional playing career.

Notorious man-about-town Walter Hagan was infamous for his tardiness, among other things.

At the 1936 Masters, Hagan was paired with Japanese golfers Chick Chin and Torchy Toda. Hiroshi Saito, Japan's ambassador to the United States, traveled from Washington to watch his two countrymen perform.

Ambassador Saito, along with Chin and Toda, arrived at the first tee 15 minutes prior to their 12:30 p.m. starting time.

But Hagan was nowhere to be found.

At 12:32, while Chin and Toda fidgeted on the tee, Sir Walter made his grand entrance, milking the moment for all it was worth.

In the middle of the tournament one year, Clifford Roberts was alerted to the fact that some of the patrons were making so much noise on the course that they were distracting the players.

Roberts immediately climbed into a cart and drove out to identify the infidels.

When he found out the revelers were TV star Jackie Gleason and some of his cronies, Roberts asked for their badges and ordered uniformed Pinkerton guards to remove the rowdies from the grounds.

"This is Augusta National," Roberts informed Gleason. "Not Broadway."

10

Bantam Ben

"I've left my blood in every cup on that golf course."
— *Ben Hogan*

Augusta National was always a challenge to Ben Hogan, who played in 25 Masters.

In 1942, often-grumpy, highly competitive 5-foot-8 Bantam Ben lost the championship by one stroke in an 18-hole playoff with Byron Nelson.

After shooting a first-round 67, Nelson proudly announced, "I've discovered a secret about playing this course. I don't want to let the other players in on it, but if I win the tournament, I'll tell you Sunday night."

The next morning, Hogan, who had been informed of Lord Byron's remarks, approached Nelson's wife at breakfast.

"I don't want to appear nosey, Louise," Hogan said, "but by any chance did Byron talk in his sleep last night?"

Four years later, Hogan three-putted the final green at Augusta National to give Herman Keiser the 1946 Masters crown.

In February, 1949, Hogan and his wife Valerie were returning to their Fort Worth, Texas, home from the Phoenix Open when their car was struck head-on by a Greyhound bus that was running late and hurtling down the wrong side of the road in an effort to pass a slow-moving truck.

Instinctively, Hogan hurled his body across that of his wife. Hogan's pelvis, ankle and several ribs were broken. He suffered extensive internal injuries.

At one point, doctors doubted that Hogan would live. Newspapers across the country hastily prepared his obituary. At best, he probably would never walk again, much less play golf.

After two months, Hogan left the hospital, nearly blind in his left eye, with both legs battered and his left shoulder permanently damaged.

Five months later, he was hitting golf shots. On Dec. 10, he played 18 holes. Eleven months after the crash, Hogan was back, competing in the Los Angeles Open.

He had to soak his legs each morning, then wrap them tightly to reduce the swelling. He suffered from cramps and was frequently in pain.

Sixteen months after his tragic accident, Hogan defied medical science by winning the 1950 U.S. Open.

Earlier that year, Hogan had found himself two shots off the lead after the first three rounds at the Masters, but finished with a 76 to open the door for his free-spirited friend, Jimmy Demaret.

Finally, in 1951, still recovering from his near-fatal crash two years earlier, Hogan conquered Augusta National for the first time.

He arrived 10 days before the start of the tournament and hit thousands of balls in practice to prepare. Hogan was not about to be denied.

At the green jacket ceremony, Bobby Jones called Hogan's comeback one of the greatest in the history of sports.

"I got a big bang out of it," Hogan told the crowd. "If I never win again, I'll be satisfied. I've had my full share of golfing luck."

Two years later, in a season in which he was only able to play in six tournaments because of his deteriorated physical condition and lack of stamina, Hogan won his second Masters—one of five victories, including three majors, in just six starts that year.

"The only emotion Ben (Hogan) shows in defeat is surprise," Demaret once noted. "You see, he expects to win."

Hogan's victory at the 1953 Masters was, even by his demanding standards, the best golf he ever played.

Having cheated death four years earlier in that 1949 crash, Hogan posted rounds of 70-69-66-69 to lower the existing Masters record by five shots and become the first man to post three rounds under 70 in the same tournament.

Only two bogeys at the end of his opening round marred an otherwise flawless four days.

"I hope to come back next year and play the same caliber of golf," Hogan said.

"If you do," replied his playing partner, Byron Nelson, "you'll be on your own."

Ben Hogan

After Bobby Jones retired in 1930, the term "Grand Slam" wasn't uttered in a game of golf again for 30 years, even though Hogan won the Masters, U.S. Open and British Open in 1953.

Qualifying for the British Open at Carnoustie, Scotland, that year coincided with the PGA Championship at Birmingham (Michigan) Country Club. And in those days, everyone, even players of Hogan's stature, had to qualify for the British Open. Even the great Hogan couldn't be at both places at the same time and supersonic trans-Atlantic jets were far in the future.

Hogan, still recovering from his earlier car crash, had entered just five tournaments that year, winning four up to that point. Now he had a choice to make. And, although after his accident Hogan disliked traveling any more than was absolutely necessary, he made it.

Hogan skipped the PGA Championship and traveled to Scotland three weeks early to accustom himself to the golf course, the weather, and the smaller British ball. It was Hogan's first and only British Open.

Nobody even mentioned the possibility of a Grand Slam.

Sam Snead defeated Hogan, 70 to 71, in an 18-hole playoff to win the 1954 Masters.

Before the two men teed off, Snead asked Hogan if he wanted to privately agree to split the purse, regardless of what happened on the golf course—a practice that was not uncommon in those days.

"That was a thing we often did in playoff situations," Snead recalled. "I felt it was fair enough."

Hogan took a couple of deep drags on his cigarette, then replied: "Let's play."

Hogan had no intention of splitting the prize money because he didn't believe he could be beaten.

"Hogan gave away less about himself than anyone I ever knew," Snead remembered. "He wished me luck on the first tee and then he just froze. You always felt there was nothing in the world important to him except his ball and how he would get it around the golf course."

Paired with Claude Harmon in the 1947 Masters, Hogan knocked his tee shot within 14 feet of the pin on Augusta's always-tricky par-3 12th hole and was apparently deep in thought when Harmon bounced his ball into the cup for a hole-in-one.

Hogan made his birdie and when the two men reached the 13th tee, Ben teed up his ball and prepared to hit first.

"You know, Claude," Hogan said, "that's the first time I've ever birdied that hole."

"But Ben," Harmon replied, "I have the honor. I made a 1!"

Hogan had been so engrossed in his own game, he didn't notice.

After missing the cut at the 1957 Masters because of poor putting, Hogan retired to the clubhouse and suggested that putting should no longer be a part of the game.

"If I had my way," Hogan grumbled, "every golf green would be made into a huge funnel. You hit the funnel and the ball would roll down a pipe into the hole.

"I've always considered that golf is one game," Hogan added, "and putting is another."

Hogan dreamed up the idea of the annual Past Champions Dinner and served as the early master of ceremonies.

Eventually Hogan stopped coming to the dinners and Byron Nelson assumed the role of emcee.

11

Slammin' Sammy

"I could always raise my game another notch or two for (Ben) Hogan."

— Sam Snead

When he was younger, sweet-swinging, remarkably limber Sam Snead would walk into the annual Past Champions Dinner during Masters Week and kick the waist-high Augusta National seal on the clubhouse library door.

It became part of the Tuesday night tradition.

Without warning one year, Snead walked through the door and announced: "The old man can't do it anymore."

Fitness fanatic Gary Player groaned, "Man, I never thought I'd see the day when the great Sambo couldn't kick that door seal."

Immediately, Arnold Palmer challenged Player.

"I'll bet $100 he can kick it if he tries again," Palmer said.

Snead, who long ago had earned a reputation as quite a hustler, walked out of the room, came in again and kicked the seal, just as he had always done.

Reportedly, Palmer and Snead then split Player's $100.

Snead, who played a couple holes of a 1942 practice round in his bare feet to attract attention to himself, won his first of three Masters titles in 1949, and his seventh and last major in 1954, when he edged Ben Hogan in a dramatic Masters playoff, 70 to 71.

To this day, that remains Snead's favorite Augusta memory.

"I could always raise my game another notch or two for Hogan," Snead explained.

By the way, those two practice holes that Snead played in his bare feet? He birdied both of them.

Before he made his Masters debut, Snead received a personal invitation to travel to Augusta to play a round with legendary Masters founder Bobby Jones. Remember, this was in the 1930s.

"Up until that time I had never been on an airplane," Snead recalled years later. "I was convinced that I didn't want to fly. But it was an opportunity to play with an idol.

"We boarded one of those open-cockpit models. We were going from Greensboro to Augusta, which today, in modern jets, you don't worry about a bit. But there were no safety devices then, such as radar. The pilot navigated his way using a Shell Oil road map that sat in his lap! He would spot landmarks by peering out of the airplane and checking them off on the map."

In 1949, Snead became the first Masters champion awarded a green jacket.

With Ben Hogan sidelined by a near-fatal head-on collision with a bus in February, Snead was finally able to snap out of his streak of near-misses and bad luck at Augusta.

After opening with lackluster rounds of 73-75—the highest 36-hole total ever to lead to a Masters victory— Snead rebounded with back-to-back 67s, which stood as the best Masters finish until Jack Nicklaus shot 64-69 on the final two rounds in 1965.

Snead—who had grown up in West Virginia and sported an Appalachian accent as well as a snappy fedora— was greeted by Great Britain's Duke of Windsor, the first member of England's royal family to visit golf's most regal tournament.

Snead fired his caddie, a man named O'Brien, after the 1953 Masters.

"I don't want you to caddy for me ever again," Snead ordered.

Three years later, when Snead arrived at Augusta National, O'Brien suddenly appeared at his side.

"I asked him if he didn't remember I had fired him," Snead explained. "And he said, 'Mister Snead, you can't get rid of me that easy.'"

When Snead's putting touch deserted him, Slammin' Sammy began to putt croquet-style.

When Snead arrived in Augusta for the 1949 Masters, Bobby Jones made it clear he did not approve.

"Sam, stop that," Jones ordered. "That doesn't look like golf."

Sam Snead

To which Snead, who had changed his putting style the previous week and had won the Greensboro Open as a result, replied: "Bob, nobody asks how you looked, just how you shot!"

Snead always suspected that Jones influenced the USGA to later prohibit players from standing behind their lines and putting croquet-style.

Snead, and others, simply moved off their line and continued putting in a manner that is today known and accepted as sidesaddle.

Prior to the start of the 1958 Masters, Snead strolled into the locker and asked Ben Hogan if he had a game lined up that afternoon.

When Hogan replied that he didn't, Snead suggested the two men might get something going.

"Sure," said Hogan. "I'll take (Ken) Venturi and we'll play anyone in the world."

"I can find an easier game than that," Snead said, walking away."

In 1973, Snead was watching the final round of the Masters on television in the antebellum clubhouse when his nephew, J.C. Snead, who was battling Tommy Aaron for the tournament lead, reached the 12th hole.

Boldly, Sam predicted that J.C. would knock his tee shot into Rae's Creek because, in Sam's opinion, he had chosen the wrong club.

J.C. Snead hit the ball into the water and eventually lost the championship to Aaron by one stroke.

In 1990, Snead tied for first place in the Par-3 Tournament that is conducted on Wednesday each year, before the Masters begins.

No small feat, since Snead was 78 and plagued by poor eyesight at the time.

One year, paired with young South African Bobby Cole in a practice round, Snead pointed to the lofty pines that towered above the left corner of the dogleg on the par-5, 13th hole.

"When I was your age, I used to knock the ball over the trees and then hit a short iron to the green," Snead boasted.

Never one to back away from a challenge, Cole drove his ball high into the air, but straight into the trees.

"I can't hit the ball over those trees, Sam," the exasperated younger golfer said, shaking his head. "How were you able to do it?"

"Easy," replied Snead, chortling. "When I was your age, those trees were only about 30 feet high."

12

Hole of Vultures, and Other Horrors

"The first time you see it (Augusta National), it looks like the most inviting course you've ever seen. You think: 'I can play this.' Then you play it a few times and you start scratching your head. Augusta National gives you plenty of room to hang yourself."

— *Ben Crenshaw*

On the first round of the 1980 Masters, long-hitting Tom Weiskopf—who had finished second four times in the tournament—lofted a 7-iron over the creek on No. 12. But the ball hit short of the green and rolled back into the drink. "It was a pretty good shot," Weiskopf insisted later.

He dropped a ball short of Rae's Creek, pitched his second shot over the water and then watched it, too, roll back into the creek.

Then, incredibly, Weiskopf knocked his next three shots into the stream before finally reaching the green, where he promptly two-putted.

If you're scoring at home, that added up to 13. In the locker room, one of the players sarcastically suggested Weiskopf had just "shot his age."

Jeanne Weiskopf, who was following her husband's plight from the gallery, broke down and began to cry.

A family friend put his arm around her and tried to console her.

"Jeanne," he said, "you don't suppose he's using new balls, do you?"

Unbelievably, the next afternoon, Weiskopf arrived at the scene of Thursday's massacre, and splashed two more balls into the creek to take a seven.

What was maybe even more amazing was the fact that in 12 previous Masters tournaments, Weiskopf had never once hit the water on No. 12.

Officially, the par-3 12th hole at Augusta National, located in the heart of "Amen Corner," along Rae's

Creek, and famed for its often-swirling winds, is called the "Golden Bell." Sounds harmless enough.

In fact, it is one of the most picturesque spots on the postcard-perfect golf course.

And one of the most cruel. When Augusta National was under construction, two tractors and eight mules became stuck in the mud there.

Gary Player called it the "Hole of Vultures." Fuzzy Zoeller labeled it "the spookiest par 3 in golf." Lloyd Mangrum claimed it is "the meanest little hole in the world." Jack Nicklaus called it, "the hardest tournament hole in golf."

It has been suggested more hope has been abandoned on the 12th hole at Augusta than on the decks of the Titanic.

Arnold Palmer triple-bogeyed the hole on the final round in 1959, and it cost him what would have been his fifth Masters crown. In his first year as a professional, Dow Finsterwald made an unsightly 11 on the 12th hole.

Sam Snead once got so angry after making an eight on the 12th hole, that he withdrew from the tournament. A double-bogey on No. 12 cost Jack Nicklaus the Masters in 1981, when he finished two strokes behind Tom Watson.

Shortly after he became president, Dwight Eisenhower, playing a round with Clifford Roberts, drove his tee shot onto a sand bar in Rae's Creek.

When Ike climbed down the bank to get his ball, he sank down well past his knees in what eventually was determined to be quicksand.

Two Secret Service agents had to jump into the water to pull the president to safety.

"The Masters," Ken Venturi observed, speaking from personal experience, "doesn't start until the back nine on Sunday."

Doug Sanders knocked the ball into the water on the 16th hole in 1966, made five, and lost the tournament by two strokes.

"I don't think I have ever liked water since," Sanders said. "I don't think I drank water for 10 years."

At the conclusion of his final round in the 1998 Masters, David Duval felt certain that, at 8-under-par, he would at the very least be in a playoff for a green jacket, probably against Fred Couples.

Fred Couples

After signing his scorecard, verifying his final round 67, Duval was whisked away to the sanctuary of the "Bobby Jones Cabin," not far from the 10th tee, to collect his wits and prepare for a possible playoff—or, better still, the traditional green jacket ceremony.

Along with his girlfriend, his caddie, and his agent, Duval struggled to stay composed and focused on the challenge ahead as he nervously watched on TV while Couples and Mark O'Meara prepared to play the fateful, final hole.

A graphic appeared on the TV screen, indicating that O'Meara now also was 8-under.

"Isn't he minus-7?" a nervous Duval asked.

"He birdied 17," Augusta National chairman Jack Stephens said.

Stunned, Duval sat, in silence, as O'Meara then sunk his 20-foot birdie putt on 18 to win the tournament.

"We'll look forward to seeing you again next year," Stephens said, as he rushed off to congratulate the winner.

Duval, an empty-handed second, felt as if he had just been kicked in the stomach. Months later, he conceded that merely thinking about the moment made his belly ache all over again.

"Never, ever, have I felt like that at the end of a golf tournament," he confessed.

Until 1950, Jim Ferrier's main claim to fame occurred in 1947 when he defeated Chick Harbert to win the PGA Championship at Plum Hollow Country Club in Detroit—despite striking seven spectators with wild shots.

With six holes to play in the 1950 Masters, Ferrier, who played with a peculiar swing due to a childhood accident, was leading the likes of Ben Hogan, Byron Nelson and Sam Snead by three or more strokes.

But he bogeyed five of the last six holes, opening the door for smartly dressed Jimmy Demaret.

Ken Venturi was a 24-year-old amateur in 1956 when he led the Masters by four strokes after the first three rounds, despite steadily increasing scores of 66, 69, and 75.

Paired with Sam Snead on that windy Sunday, Venturi soared to an 80 on the slick, fast Augusta National greens.

"It was inexperience," Venturi admitted years later. "And nerves. Strictly nerves. I'm not afraid to admit it."

Twenty years later, with Raymond Floyd leading the 1976 Masters by eight shots entering the final round, Venturi—by then a CBS TV commentator—was asked if it was possible for anyone to overcome such a lead.

"Sure, it's conceivable," Venturi said. "I know someone who lost an eight-shot lead in the Masters once. Matter of fact, I saw him in the mirror this morning when I was shaving."

Argentina's Roberto De Vicenzo fired a 65 on the final round of the 1968 Masters to tie Bob Goalby and apparently force an 18-hole playoff the next day.

But Tommy Aaron, who was keeping De Vicenzo's scorecard, inadvertently credited Roberto with a par 4 on the 17th hole, instead of the birdie 3 which he had actually made.

De Vicenzo didn't notice and signed the incorrect card. Actually Roberto, who had little formal schooling and was not particularly proficient in mathematics, rarely bothered to check his score.

Under golf's rules, he was stuck with the higher total and Goalby was awarded the green jacket by default.

"What a stupid I am," De Vicenzo muttered.

Raymond Floyd

"I play maybe 30 years, maybe all over the world. I sign so many scorecards, and I never be wrong. I feel sorry for me. I think I am too old to have another chance like this."

He was right.

The 1968 scoring snafu haunted Bob Goalby, Roberto De Vicenzo and Tommy Aaron throughout the remainder of their careers.

Goalby, the tainted champion who had gone birdie-birdie-eagle on the 13th, 14th and 15th holes to shoot a final-round 66, never did receive the credit he deserved as Masters champ.

"I had just played the best golf of my career," Goalby said. "But you had to feel sorry for Roberto."

"I knew that people would make me the heavy, people are uninformed about the rules," Aaron said. "It was a terrible thing and, of course, I feel badly about it. But if you play by the rules, well, it's not my fault. He (De Vicenzo) is responsible for his scorecard."

Aaron rebounded to win a Masters of his own in 1973. "Every year something magical seems to happen at the Masters," said the surprise winner, who had survived only three cuts in the two months of PGA Tour play prior to Augusta that year.

De Vicenzo's blunder was not the first in Masters play.

In 1953, Sam Snead signed a scorecard on which his playing partner, Byron Nelson, had mistakenly put down a 4 when Snead, in fact, had made a 3.

Amateur Charlie Coe was disqualified for signing an incorrect scorecard that gave him a lower score in 1957.

Jim Turnesa signed for a 5 when he had actually made a 4 on the seventh hole in 1961, and as a result, missed the cut by a single stroke.

On the first hole of the 1968 Masters, Marty Fleckman sliced his tee shot into a nearby parking lot.

"Should I play a provisional ball?" Fleckman asked a tournament official.

"I don't know," the official replied. "Nobody has ever hit it there before."

In 1978, Tommy Nakajima of Japan took a very unlucky 13 on the par-5 13th hole.

In an interview afterward, Nakajima was asked if he had lost his composure.

"No lose composure," he said. "Lose count."

After burly 1982 Masters champion Craig Stadler shot an opening-round 79 in 1998, a reporter asked him if he had a particular number in mind for Friday's second round at Augusta.

"Nine-thirty," Stadler growled in reply.

"Nine-thirty?" the puzzled reporter persisted.

"Yeah," Stadler shot back. "The 9:30 flight out of here tomorrow night."

13

The Squire

"Wherever I go, people say, 'That's the man who got the double eagle.' Actually, it was just a piece of luck."
— *Gene Sarazen*

The sudden retirement of Masters founder Bobby Jones in 1930 left Gene Sarazen as the best golfer in the game.

"When he (Sarazen) is in the right mood, he is probably the greatest scorer in the game," Jones himself once wrote.

"The Squire," as Sarazen was known because of his lack of his height and his many real estate holdings, won nine tournaments in 1930. And by the time Augusta National was completed and the first Masters was staged in 1934, Sarazen had one British Open title, two U.S. Opens, and three PGA championships to his credit.

So how come Sarazen was conspicuous by his absence from the inaugural Masters in 1934?

Sarazen—who had changed his name from Saraceni because he didn't want people to mistake him for a concert violinist—was invited in '34, but he inadvertently tossed the invitation into the trash.

"I remember the return address on the invitation had (Masters co-founder) Cliff Roberts' name on the envelope," recalled Sarazen, who died in 1999 at the age of 97.

"I said, 'Aw, the hell with this.' I thought it was some kind of promotion to sell stocks or real estate. Why the hell do I want to play in a tournament sponsored by a Wall Street broker?"

Besides, Sarazen wasn't inclined to cancel his profitable overseas exhibition tour with trick-shot artist Joe Kirkwood for some first-year tournament in a sleepy little resort town in East Georgia.

"But the invitation the next year said 'Bobby Jones' on it," Sarazen recalled. "Now that was something."

Despite the impact of Bobby Jones' return, the Masters remained a small tournament at a small club in a small town.

Gene Sarazen

But in 1935, Gene Sarazen put Augusta National on the map.

On the par-5 15th hole of the final day of the 1935 Masters, Sarazen trailed Craig Wood—the club pro from Winged Foot in New York, who had already completed his round—by three strokes.

In the clubhouse, Wood was accepting congratulations from fellow players and answering questions about his round. A check for the winner's share of $1,500 had already been made out in Wood's name.

But Sarazen wasn't quite through.

On No. 15, Sarazen drove his tee shot down the center of the fairway, 230 yards from the green.

"Come on, Gene, hit it will ya?" Sarazen's playing partner, playboy Walter Hagen, implored, as the normally fast-playing Sarazen pondered his second shot. "I've got a date tonight."

It was a cold, wet afternoon. According to Sarazen, there were fewer than 25 well-chilled fans in his gallery. But Bobby Jones himself was waiting, watching near the 15th green.

Sarazen's caddie suggested a three-wood, but "The Squire" reasoned that, although he probably wouldn't be able to reach the green with a four-wood, a three-wood probably wouldn't hold the green.

Sarazen trusted his instincts, opted for a four-wood, closed the club face to decrease the loft, and blasted the ball toward the pin.

"Not until I pulled the ball out of the cup did I realize what I'd done," Sarazen later admitted.

Double eagle!

"I felt no elation," Sarazen said. "It came too quick."

The next day, headline writers called it "The Shot Heard 'Round The World," and newspapers reported that "a gallery of 2,000 cheered."

"That shot," Sarazen later admitted, "was the greatest thrill I've ever had on a golf course."

With that one remarkable shot, Sarazen had tied Wood. But he still had three holes to play.

Sarazen pared the final three holes, then whipped Wood 144-149 in a grueling 36-hole playoff the following day.

Clifford Roberts congratulated "The Squire" and gave him a $50 bonus for having had to play 108 holes to win the tournament.

Sarazen often said that during the course of the rest of his life he encountered "about 20,000 people who claimed they saw that shot."

But it was 32 years between Sarazen's historic double eagle in '35 and the next double-eagle at Augusta, which was recorded by Bruce Devlin in the 1967 Masters.

At the 1935 Masters, after firing an opening-round 68 to tie Ray Mangrum for the early lead, Gene Sarazen suddenly awoke in the middle of the night in his downtown Augusta hotel room to see a shadowy figure standing at the foot of his bed, staring at him.

"Who are you?" the drowsy golfer demanded. "What do you want?"

The shadowy figure said nothing and Sarazen began to get nervous. Fearing foul play, he reached for his driver in the golf bag near his bed.

Finally a woman's voice shattered the silence.

"I beg your pardon," the embarrassed woman said. "I must be in the wrong room."

Gene Sarazen played in 34 Masters before retiring in 1973. Beginning in 1981, he joined Byron Nelson and Sam Snead as honorary starters at Augusta.

"Gene was kind of like an old firehorse," Nelson said. "He was ready to go all the time. He will be remembered forever, as long as golf is being played, for the way he played, for the competitor he was."

14

Lord Byron

"When someone asks me what was the most important win of all for me, I never hesitate. It was the 1937 Masters, the one that really gave me confidence in myself."
— *Byron Nelson*

Byron Nelson's 32 on the back nine on Sunday's final round at the 1937 Masters catapulted him to a two-shot victory over Ralph Guldahl.

"That 32 did more for my career at that time than anything," admitted Lord Byron who won a total of 52 professional tournaments. "I realized then my game would stand up under pressure and I could make good decisions under difficult circumstances. It was the turning point.

"When someone asks me what was the most important win of all for me, I never hesitate. It was the

1937 Masters, the one that really gave me confidence in myself."

In 1938, the year after young Nelson won his first Masters, he approached tournament co-founder Clifford Roberts, who had made his fortune in the stock market, and asked if Roberts could recommend some stocks he might buy.

"Well, what do you have now?" Roberts inquired.

Nelson replied that he had a few thousand dollars invested in some penny stocks.

"Where'd you get those dogs?" snapped Roberts, who proceeded to inform Nelson that he normally didn't bother with accounts under $1 million.

Remember, this was 1938.

By the way, Roberts' investment company, the Reynolds Company, later became Dean Witter Reynolds.

Although Nelson won 26 PGA tournaments in 1944-45—including 11 in a row between March and August, 1945—some dismissed his accomplishments, noting that many of the day's best golfers were away,

Byron Nelson

serving in the military. Nelson was exempt because he was a hemophiliac.

Because of World War II restrictions, only 42 golfers traveled to Augusta for the 1942 Masters.

After trailing by three strokes after the first five holes of their 18-hole playoff on Monday, Byron Nelson rallied to defeat Ben Hogan, 69 to 70.

It marked the only time those two legends ever went head-to-head in a playoff and, according to Nelson, "at least 25 of the pros who played in the Masters stayed to watch the playoff."

As Cliff Roberts noted: "I don't believe any day of golf ever had more attention from golf people themselves."

To show his appreciation for their performance, Clifford Roberts sent both Nelson and Hogan bonus checks for $200—which was the total amount the Masters made from ticket sales for the playoff.

15

Destiny, Fate, and Dreams

"I held the Masters in awe when I was young—and I hold it in awe now."

— Arnold Palmer

Ben Crenshaw didn't master Augusta National until 1984, on his 12th try.

The key came on the 10th hole of the final round when Crenshaw, who had begun the day two shots behind Tom Kite, sank a tremendous 60-foot birdie putt to take a two-shot lead.

"From where I was standing," Crenshaw said, in describing that putt, "my caddie Carl Jackson, who was tending to the flagstick, looked as if he were in a different part of Georgia."

When he finally donned his first green jacket, the popular, emotional Crenshaw went out of his way to thank the Masters' galleries that had been so supportive, both during that tournament and throughout his career.

"If I could cut out a piece of my heart, I'd give it to you," Crenshaw said.

When Crenshaw won again in 1995, he was convinced he had been destined to win that year because his close friend and golfing mentor, 90-year-old Harvey Penick, had passed away the previous week.

"It was kind of like I felt his hand on my shoulder, guiding me along," said Crenshaw, who shot 274.

"I believe in fate," he added. "Fate has dictated another championship here, as it has done so many times."

In February, 1933, a year before the first Masters tournament, as Augusta National was struggling to get off the ground, one of the guests invited to play the new course was a Wall Street lawyer named Prescott S. Bush.

Bush also happened to be chairman of the United States Golf Association's tournament committee. In addition, Bush's father-in-law was George H. Walker, the former president of the USGA and the man for whom the Walker Cup had been named.

Eventually, Prescott S. Bush's son and grandson would both become Presidents of the United States.

Nick Faldo carded a final-round 65 to tie Scott Hoch for the lead in 1989, then sank a 25-foot birdie putt on the second playoff hole to win the tournament.

"It felt like destiny," he said. "I felt like I made history."

The next year, Faldo rallied on the back nine on Sunday to force another playoff. And again Faldo prevailed in overtime to join Jack Nicklaus (1965-66) as the Masters' only back-to-back champions.

As a youngster, Augusta native Larry Mize would stand on the ninth fairway of the Augusta Country Club and peer through the wire fence at adjacent Augusta National.

When he was 14, Mize got a job putting the red and green numbers up on the scoreboard overlooking the third hole during the Masters.

But he steadfastly refused all off-season invitations to play the hallowed course.

He dreamed that someday he, too, would be permitted to play in the Masters and he didn't want to spoil it.

"I dreamed of winning it a lot of times," Mize admitted. "I guess, in my dreams, I've won it about every way I could."

In 1987, Mize's dream came true in dramatic fashion.

The night before Sunday's final round, Mize lay in bed, pondering the position he found himself in.

"I remember thinking, 'I don't know what's going to happen tomorrow, but I feel real good about where I stand right now,'" Mize later recalled. "'There are some big names in there with me, but maybe I can somehow slip in there.'"

When Mize arrived at the course Sunday he admittedly was nervous. "But nervous is good when you have a chance to win at Augusta," he rationalized.

Hours later, the slender golfer ousted Seve Ballesteros and Greg Norman in a sudden-death showdown, bouncing a chip shot into the 11th hole from 140 feet away to win the tournament on the second playoff hole.

"It was in all the way," Mize said.

"It's funny when I look back at the video and see me chip it and then freeze in my follow-through," he continued. "I wish I could have a front view so that I could see my eyes getting bigger and bigger the closer the ball got to the hole. I just threw up my arms and started running.

"You have big dreams as a child," Mize added. "Mine came true that day."

On the first tee of a stop on the 2000 PGA Tour, Mize was introduced as "the 1967 Masters champion."

"If I had won the Masters in 1967," Mize pointed out, "I would have been nine years old."

After near misses in 1937, when he was nipped by hard-charging Byron Nelson, and in 1938, when he was outdueled by Henry Picard, Ralph Guldahl shot a 33 on the back nine to win the 1939 Masters by one shot over Sam Snead, who shot a 280 and looked like a certain winner entering the final round.

In spite of Guldahl's success, one year later, after playing in the 1940 U.S. Open, he retired from tournament golf.

Swashbuckling young Seve Ballesteros was arguably the most able of the foreign golfers who dominated the Masters from 1980 through 1996, winning the tournament 10 times.

Ballesteros grew up alongside a golf course in northern Spain. His uncle Ramon finished sixth behind Jack Nicklaus in the 1965 Masters. Seve often caddied for his older brother, Manuel, who turned pro in 1969. Seve himself became Spain's youngest pro golfer ever when he turned pro at age 16.

Ballesteros joined the European Tour in 1974, and three years later he was being hailed as the world's most exciting player since Arnold Palmer.

Famed for his powerful although sometimes erratic driver, Seve soon became equally renowned for his clever recovery shots.

But, incredibly, on the day the dashing young Ballesteros—who spoke little or no English—won the 1980 Masters, Spanish national radio began its newscast with a bulletin about a Spanish swimming record that had just been broken.

No mention was made of the Spaniard had just posted the lowest score ever by an international player at the Masters, a 13-under-par 275.

Seve Ballesteros

As he was exiting Augusta National, Arnold Palmer was once asked what he thought about Ballesteros.

"I used to play like that," Palmer said.

Three birdies and an eagle on the final round enabled Ballesteros to win the 1983 Masters.

Noted Tom Kite: "That's like driving a Ferrari and everybody else out there is driving a Chevrolet."

Coming into the 1986 Masters, Ballesteros complained that he had played only nine competitive rounds all year because of the recent death of his father, and as a result had won very little money.

"Only $90," Ballesteros quipped. "And all of that was practice round bets with (Ben) Crenshaw and (Gary) Player."

In position to make birdie on the par-3 16th hole at the 1986 Masters, Ballesteros barely tapped his putt, then watched it roll 20 feet past the cup on the slick green.

Coming back, Seve took nearly a full swing—and left his second putt 10 feet short.

Then he missed his putt for bogey and ended up with a four-putt, double-bogey 5.

When he was asked to explain the disaster, Seve, in his Spanish accent, said: "I mees, I mees, I mees, I make."

Then he returned to the champions' locker room where he suggested, in very understandable English, that the offending 16th green ought to be blown up.

No player has ever won the Wednesday Par-3 Contest and the Masters Tournament in the same year.

Raymond Floyd (1990) and Chip Beck (1993) came the closest, each winning the Par-3 before finishing second in the main event.

Davis Love Jr. won a crystal vase for posting the low score (69) on the first round of the 1964 Masters. On April 13, the day after Love returned home from Augusta, his son, Davis the Third, was born.

Davis Love III's best finish in the Masters came in 1995 when he placed second behind Ben Crenshaw and in again 1999, when he was runner-up to Jose Maria Olazabal.

"That was a very good score (13 under 275)," Love said of his effort in '95. "The only reason I could feel good about finishing second was because Ben won. And that's how I still feel. I'll always remember that score."

16

The Shark

"I feel good here. I like the place. I like the atmosphere. It's one of the few golf courses in the world that can do that for me. Once you get here, it's heaven. It's golf."
— *Greg Norman*

If Greg Norman played professional football instead of golf, he would be a Minnesota Viking or a Buffalo Bill. Often the bridesmaid, but never the bride. Close so many times, but no cigar.

No player has experienced more heartbreak and disappointment at Augusta National than Norman. No one has had more chances to conquer the storied course—or more gut-gnawing near-misses.

"It's just a shame that he hasn't won it," said a sympathetic Tiger Woods, who won his first Masters title on his first professional try while Norman failed in his first 21 chances.

"I want to see Greg win the Masters," agreed two-time champ Jose Maria Olazabal. "Then he can retire in peace."

Norman has made millions selling his extensive line of golf clothing, but all the money in the world can't buy him one green jacket.

However, Norman is not one to feel sorry for himself.

"If I thought about that, I'd go crazy," admitted the Great White Shark. "To analyze some of the situations that I've been in around here and come up with a logical answer is not logical.

"It's been one huge emotional roller coaster, no question about that," acknowledged Norman, who has finished second on three occasions, third on three others, and fourth, fifth and sixth once each.

In 1986, Norman had the Masters won until Jack Nicklaus forgot that he was 46 years old and caught The Shark from behind.

Greg Norman

The following April, the Augusta National tailors were again measuring Norman for a green jacket when little known Larry Mize somehow knocked the little white ball in the hole from 140 feet away.

A bogey at 18 cost him a chance at a possible play-off in 1989 and a bogey on 17 knocked him out in 1995.

In 1996, Norman blew a seemingly insurmountable six-stroke lead on the final day to fall to Nick Faldo by five shots in what may have been the most shocking pratfall in any major championship in golf history.

It stands, to this day, as the catastrophe against which all other golf disasters are measured.

Norman shot a final-round 78. Faldo fired a 67. In the locker room Nick Price admitted, "Nobody could believe what was happening."

"I'm not a loser," Norman sadly insisted, as the sun set on the beguiling temptress that, for him, Augusta National had become.

"It's not the end of the world. My life will continue. I've got 40 million bucks."

But no green jacket.

In 1999, tied with Jose Maria Olazabal with five holes to play, and with virtually everyone at Augusta

National that afternoon rooting for him, the White Shark was left standing forlornly at the altar once again.

When Norman eagled the 13th hole to take the lead on the final round, he could almost feel that green coat on his shoulders.

But Olazabal answered moments later with a birdie of his own and, for Norman, another gut-wrenching loss began to unfold.

It was the Nightmare on Magnolia Lane all over again as the outrageously overdue Norman bogeyed the 14th and 15th holes to squander possibly his last chance at a coveted green coat, finishing third by three strokes.

Even Olazabal was sympathetic.

"I want to win the green jacket," said Olazabal, "but Greg deserves a green jacket as much as anyone else."

However, Norman isn't one to look for pity.

"Let's not make a mountain out of a mole hill on this one," he urged.

"I've never played in front of that much excitement, not even in my home country," Norman said. "You could actually feel the energy inside the ropes. Very seldom, as an athlete, can you really feel that.

"People like to think of all the bad things that have happened to me here, but I don't," Norman insisted. "I like to think of all the good things.

"People like to talk about the bad things more than the good. But that's just the nature of life in general. People don't like to hear the good news. They like the bad news.

"I can walk to every hole and remember the good shots I hit on that hole, and to me that's the most important thing," Norman continued. "I don't let the legacy or the negative energy of this place come in and try to pollute my mind.

"Somebody asked me, if I had a magic wand to wave, what would I change? I'd change nothing."

17

Ollie

"There were times I would just daydream back to Augusta, to what it would mean to win there again. How could I top that?"

— *Jose Maria Olazabal*

His Basque countrymen call him "Ollie." His close friends call him "Chemma." But most American golf fans barely know two-time Masters champion Jose Maria Olazabal.

Most don't even know how to properly pronounce his name. It's "oh-luh-THAH-bull."

While Tiger Woods lives in an elaborate three-bedroom villa in the most exclusive, most expensive neighborhood in Orlando, Florida, the 36-year-old Olazabal, a multi-millionaire in his own right, still lives at home, with his parents, in a small fishing village.

Of course, home is a six-bedroom, five-bath, one-fitness-center palace that Olazabal built for himself and his parents, near the seventh hole of Real Club de San Sebastian in Fuenterrabia, Spain.

There his mother, Juli, cooks his meals and cleans his clothes. At least Jose Maria has his own room and bath, and, presumably, no curfew.

"In a way, I'm spoiled by my family," Olazabal admitted.

Basques are, by nature, a wary, reticent people who thrive in the remote reaches of northern Spain, protected from the prying eyes and inquiries of outsiders by the Pyrenees Mountains. They hunt and fish. They chase whales. Jai alai, handball and soccer—not golf—are their national pastimes.

It is there that Jose Maria Olazabal feels most comfortable. He treasures the silence and the solitude.

He owns one automobile. And one wristwatch.

"I'm not one for material things," said Olazabal, who enjoys walking in the mountains and listening to music. "I have simple tastes."

"He is the most private major champion in the world," said Jose Maria's agent and confidant, Sergio Gomez.

Jose Maria Olazabal

While Woods demands top dollar and reaps more than $100 million a year from his endorsements alone, Olazabal signed a contract with MacGregor for one-fifth of what a competitor was offering.

While Woods hangs out with Michael Jordan, Olazabal's best friend is his sister.

While it sometimes seemed as if Woods' father, Earl, was everywhere, Olazabal's father, Gaspar, is so afraid of flying that he refuses to travel to Augusta to watch his son play.

Instead, Gasper Olazabal, a greenskeeper like his father before him, watches the Masters tournament on television each year. When his son won in 1994 and again in 1999, Gasper walked outside his home and fired his hunting rifle into the air, then set off a few fireworks.

The saga of Jose Maria Olazabal is truly one of golf's heartwarming stories.

Unable to walk four years earlier, in so much pain because of a misdiagnosed back ailment that he was often forced to crawl from his bed to the bathroom, Olazabal completed his comeback and defied the odds in 1999 by upstaging sudden fan-favorite Greg Norman to claim his second green jacket.

"I really believe things are meant to happen sometimes," an emotional Olazabal said, with tears in his eyes, his voice quivering. "And (1999) was meant to happen the way it happened."

Initially, Olazabal was misdiagnosed with rheumatoid arthritis in both feet that made the mere act of walking excruciating. Playing golf was out of the question. There was no known cure.

Depressed, Olazabal refused to see his friends or his fellow golfers on the European Tour. He became a recluse. As much as possible, he even avoided his parents, although they lived together in the same house.

"It was hard for them, knowing the situation," he admitted. "You just had to look in their eyes.

"I reached the point where I couldn't walk at all," he recalled. "I had to crawl. I figured that I was done, that I'd never have a chance to play again. I thought I would end my life in a wheelchair.

"During the night, just before falling asleep, I started to think about it. I did cry, but not much. It gets you down very low, very low. We really don't know our limits as human beings until we're faced with something as bad as that.

"I remember reading things that were so silly, like I had AIDs or I was fat," Olazabal continued. "The best thing to do was just try not to say a single word. You just try to hide your emotions."

Olazabal was out of action for 18 months. In September, 1996, on a desperation trip to Germany, a doctor informed Jose Maria that the problem was not with his feet at all, but rather with his back.

Skeptical, but barely able to stand, Olazabal asked the doctor when he might be able to play golf again.

By February or March, the doctor said.

"I want to play the Masters," Olazabal replied. "I want to be there."

The doctor gave Olazabal some injections in his lower back and put him on a rigorous training program.

"According to the doctor, the problem was caused in my lower back, between a couple of vertebrae that were pinching some of the nerves," Olazabal explained. "No one had ever looked there."

The treatment was painful but by February, five months after his first session with the German doctor, Olazabal was running on the beaches near his home.

Gradually, the pain began to subside. He began swinging his golf clubs again.

In April, 1997, Olazabal finished an exhilarating 12th in the Masters behind wunderkind Tiger Woods.

Olazabal was only two when he picked up a golf club, a rusty putter, for the first time. One of the members at the aristocratic course where both of Jose Maria's parents worked gave it to the youngster to keep him occupied and out of the way.

Eventually, he accumulated a 4-wood, then a 5-iron, a 7-iron and a 9-iron that had been discarded by wealthy members. Jose Maria hit the ball left-handed until he was five, then became a right-hander.

"At that time, golf was not very popular in Spain," Olazabal recalled. "The members only came on weekends. The rest of the time, I had the whole course to myself. I learned the game on my own."

While Olazabal's parents worked at the golf course —his father caring for the greens, his mother cooking and cleaning—young Jose Maria taught himself to play.

"To go into town, to see other children, would be a long bike ride away," Olazabal recalled. "The golf course was right there."

Olazabal won the British Amateur in 1984, which earned him an invitation to the '85 Masters.

Fellow Spaniard Seve Ballesteros, then the No. 1-ranked player in the world, gave Olazabal a videotape of his own 1983 Masters victory.

Olazabal was amazed at what he saw. Augusta National was so green, so pristine, not at all like the craggy terrain Jose Maria was accustomed to in Spain.

"This is heaven," Olazabal said.

Olazabal was at a loss for words after winning the 1994 Masters. "There are no words to express what I feel in a moment like this," he said.

When Olazabal returned home, he was invited to meet Juan Carlos, the king of Spain. Jose Maria proudly wore his green jacket to the palace.

18

Rookies

"The first time we drove in, it took about half an hour to get down Magnolia Lane because I was hanging out the window, gaping, and my wife was hanging out the other side, taking pictures. It was as if we were pulling into Valhalla or something."

— *Scott McCarron*

In 2001, 32-year-old, one-time PGA Tour winner and Masters rookie Chris DiMarco became the new Dennis Paulson, Brandel Chamblee, Jim Gallagher, Mike Donald, Robert Wrenn, and Ken Green.

He was the nobody who came out of nowhere to scorch the sacred fairways and slick greens of Augusta National on opening day.

As soon as DiMarco found out he would be making his Masters debut in 2001, he began picking the brains of every Augusta-savvy veteran he was paired with on the PGA Tour: Bernhard Langer, Fred Couples, Jose Maria Olazabal, Ernie Els, Phil Mickelson.

As things turned out, DiMarco didn't need that much advice.

"It was easy," he announced after he fired a seven-under par 65 on only his third stroll ever around the storied golf course.

"I had heard how hard this course was. Not to hit it here, not to hit it there. But if you're playing well, you're going to score well, no matter where you are."

When DiMarco arrived at Augusta National for the first time on the Monday before the 2001 Masters, he anxiously sat down in front of his locker to prepare for his first practice round on the fabled course.

It was a moment he had been waiting for, a day he had been dreaming about, his whole life.

Out of habit, DiMarco set his spikes down on the bench beside him—as he always did—while he removed his street shoes.

Immediately, a concerned attendant appeared at DiMarco's side.

"Sir," the attendant quietly informed him, "we don't put shoes on the bench at Augusta National."

"I said, 'Okay,' " DiMarco later recalled, "and I put my shoes down on the floor. He may have been just ribbing the rookie, but I didn't want to find out."

Although DiMarco refused to admit it publicly, he had to be relieved on the final round of the 2001 tournament to be paired with fellow former University of Florida Gator Mark Calcavecchio—one group behind Tiger Woods' crowded traveling circus.

Paired with Woods in the third round—when Tiger was, as usual, the center of attention as he sought to complete his sweep of the four majors—DiMarco turned to Woods as the two men were walking down the 10th fairway and asked: "You have to go through this every day?"

"Yep," Woods replied. "How do you like it?"

"You can have it, partner," DiMarco said. "It's all yours."

Late in March of 1996, Scott McCarron, who had flopped on both the Asian and Canadian circuits before he finally qualified for the PGA Tour, realized he was broke.

He had a new baby, and the loans he had taken out to support his father's apparel business were due. McCarron decided he would file bankruptcy during the 1996 Masters. After all, he had nothing better to do that week.

Instead, just when the situation appeared most bleak, McCarron won a PGA tournament in New Orleans, which put $270,000 into his empty checking account and sent him to Augusta as a rookie the following week.

"I went from a frog to a prince overnight," McCarron said.

In 1986, Shelly Green became the first female caddie in Masters history when she carried the bag belonging to her brother, outspoken rookie Ken Green.

"I was just there so he'd have somebody to talk to," she explained.

Rookie Fuzzy Zoeller thought for sure he was doomed in 1979 when he saw that both Tom Watson and Ed Sneed had knocked their balls to within 10 feet of the cup on the first hole of their three-way play-off—the first sudden-death showdown in Masters history.

"I looked at the green and wondered if there was any room for my ball," admitted Zoeller.

As it turned out, all three players missed their putts on No. 10 and Zoeller sunk an eight-footer on the next extra hole to become the first rookie to win the Masters since Gene Sarazen in 1935.

Australian Greg Chalmers, playing in his first Masters in 2001, struck a fan in the head with his tee shot on the first hole of the opening round.

The ball caromed over into the adjacent ninth fairway, from where Chalmers immediately struck another unlucky fan on the shoulder with his second shot.

As you might expect, golf is not particularly popular in Paraguay. But, after finishing a surprising sixth in

Fuzzy Zoeller

the 1999 Masters, native son Carlos Franco certainly was.

In 1999, Franco became the first South American golfer invited to the Masters since Brazilian amateur Priscilo Gonzalez Diniz in 1976.

"Before the Masters, no one in Paraguay knows Carlos Franco," said Franco. "After the Masters, Carlos Franco is bigger than the President."

Notah Begay III, who had pled guilty to drinking and driving, prepared for the 2000 Masters while confined for a week in a minimum security prison.

"Mostly, I thought about how lucky I was to be playing golf for a living," he said.

During a work-release program, Begay spent more than eight hours a day honing the golf shots he would use during his first appearance at Augusta.

"The people in there (prison) probably couldn't care less if I played in the Masters," he admitted. "They've got their own troubles."

Brandel Chamblee admitted he had heard all the "horror stories" about how intimidating August National could be before he played in his first Masters in 1999.

"I've been watching this tournament since 1975," Chamblee explained. "In the past, I usually did my taxes this week, then had some friends over for a Masters party on Sunday."

When Brent Geiberger was nine, his father, Al, invited him to hit a couple of tee shots during the annual Par-3 Contest. In 2000 the Geibergers became the ninth father-son combo in Masters history.

When Chris DiMarco, early-round surprise of the 2001 Masters, was a youngster—"8, 9, 10, back then," he recalled—he would play a game of pretend on the golf course near his Florida home.

"I'd play four balls," DiMarco explained. "One ball would be me, one would be Jack Nicklaus, one would be Arnold Palmer, and one would be Gary Player. I used to try to beat them. I always made them miss their four-footers."

While eventual champion Tiger Woods was peacefully sequestered in a palatial Augusta estate during the 2001 tournament, protected by bodyguards and his entourage, DiMarco had to share the small home he had rented with his mother and father, his two brothers, and his mother-in-law.

When Woods awoke each morning, his color-coordinated wardrobe, scripted by Nike and approved by Tiger months in advance, was already laid out for him.

When it was time for DiMarco to get dressed, shortly before dawn, he grabbed a green shirt for good luck.

"It was my first round at the Masters and, obviously, the Masters is synonymous with green," he explained.

Tom Scherrer got very little sleep the night before he shot a fine 71 in the first round of his first Masters in 2001. His infant son, Tom, kept him awake much of the night with his crying.

"I was thinking," Scherrer groaned. "'The one time in the Masters, and now you're crying.'"

19

Tiger's Buddy

"To know that Masters trophy is setting at home in my trophy cabinet, to know I'll always be invited back to Augusta National, to know my name will go down in history with some of the greatest names of all time, that's enough for me."

— *Mark O'Meara*

Middle-aged Mark O'Meara, slightly chubby, balding, and 0-for-56 in major championships up until that point, went out for dinner with fellow pro John Cook in Augusta one evening before the 1998 Masters began.

As soon as the two golfers were seated at the restaurant, an excited fan—one of the wide-eyed thou-

Mark O'Meara

sands who annually pack Augusta during Masters Week—rushed over to their table.

"Mark McCumber! Mark McCumber!" the alleged golf aficionado exclaimed, extending his hand which held a scrap of paper to be signed.

"I'm sorry, I'm Mark O'Meara," the soon-to-be-crowned Masters champion apologized.

The fan asked for O'Meara's autograph anyway.

As O'Meara was walking from the 16th green to the 17th tee on the final round of the 1998 Masters, trailing David Duval and Fred Couples with one shot, Mark turned to his caddie, Jerry Higginbotham, and said: "You know, I can make birdie on these last two holes and win this thing."

And that was exactly what he did.

"My heart was definitely racing as I walked toward the 18th green," O'Meara admitted. "I was nervous. You look at my face on the film and I don't look nervous. But I know how I felt.

"As soon as I struck that putt, when the ball was about two feet off the putter, I thought, 'Man, I hit a good putt, thank you.' I knew people watching on TV all around the world were glued on what the outcome would be.

"When the ball finally went in the hole, I was proud of myself, I was stunned a little bit, I was shocked a little bit, there was a little bit of disbelief—and a lot of joy," O'Meara added.

"When I see footage of it, watching it go in gives me more goosebumps now then it did when it went in."

Before the 41-year-old O'Meara, a career under-achiever who didn't begin playing golf until he was 13, sank his pressure-packed 20-foot birdie putt on the 72nd hole to win the 1998 Masters, his main claim to fame may have been the fact that he was Tiger Woods' best friend.

"Tiger has helped push me," O'Meara admitted, after his best buddy had slipped the green jacket over his shoulders. "His enthusiasm and tremendous desire to be a major force in golf rubs off."

O'Meara's victory, in his 15th try at Augusta, was a Masters record.

"Hey, we're talking about Mark O'Meara here," he said.

"I wouldn't classify myself as a great player. My estimate of great are players like Jack Nicklaus and Ben

Hogan and Gene Sarazen. I'm just proud to know that one time I got to wear that green jacket."

20

Only at Augusta

"It's always a special day at the Masters. Dramatics happen here. Train wrecks. Apollo launchings. Roller coaster rides. It's amazing."

— *Mark McCumber*

Jokester Fuzzy Zoeller was merely trying to be funny once again when, during the final round of Tiger Woods' 1997 Augusta runaway, he quipped: "Tell him (Woods) not to serve fried chicken at the (champions') dinner next year. Or collard greens or whatever the hell they serve."

Zoeller's ill-chosen remarks, which went largely ignored at the time and weren't actually aired until a week after the Masters was over, continue to haunt him to this day.

"I forgive him," Woods finally said, months later. "But I can't forget."

Long-driving John Daly was signing autographs between the ninth green and the 10th tee during a 1992 practice round when a man thrust a piece of paper in front of him.

Without looking up, Daly continued walking while he signed.

Only then did he realize the autograph-seeker was actually a process-server, presenting Daly with a paternity suit that had been filed against him by a former girl friend.

Disgusted, Daly handed the papers to his caddie, who stuffed them into John's golf bag as the round continued.

The first thing Daly did when he arrived at Augusta National in 2000 was go directly to the pro shop to purchase 120 golf shirts, each of which bore the coveted Masters logo, for friends back home in Arkansas.

Because Daly wasn't sure when he would be invited back.

He had good reason to be worried.

When he didn't receive an invitation to play in the tournament the following year, Daly, whose five-year Masters exemption expired in 2000, wrote tournament officials, requesting an extension.

Daly maintained that because he was unable to take advantage of all five years of the exemption he had earned by winning the 1995 British Open —Daly missed the 1997 Masters because he was in an alcohol rehabilitation clinic— he should have been granted an extra year of eligibility.

He was turned down.

In eight Masters appearances, Daly—whose power-game is tailor-made for Augusta's wide-open fairways—has made the cut seven times. His best finish has been a tie for third in 1993.

Each Masters participant is allowed to purchase 12 tickets to the tournament.

In 1989, Ken Green arrived in Augusta with a dozen friends and family members—but only five tickets. His wife, with whom Green was feuding at the time, had the other seven tickets at home in Florida, and refused to part with them.

Even though he was playing in the tournament, Green was not permitted to purchase any additional tickets. So Green smuggled his seven un-ticketed guests onto the grounds by hiding them in the back seat and in the trunk of his courtesy car.

The night before the final round of the 2000 Masters, Qass Singh, Vijay's 10-year-old son, penned a secret message on his dad's golf bag.

"Papa, trust your swing," it said.

Twenty-four hours later, Singh donned a green jacket as Masters champion.

Singh grew up in Fiji, the southeastern-most in a string of islands that stretch from India and Thailand toward Australia.

There was an airport between Singh's family home and the nearby golf course, and young Vijay had to dart across the runway, dodging airplanes, with his clubs in hand.

Vijay Singh

"Every hour there would be a flight or two," Singh explained. "You learned the busy times."

In 1998, Singh missed the cut at the Masters and was somberly driving home to Ponte Vedra Beach, Florida, when his wife, Ardena, finally decided she had heard enough.

Either stop fussing and fuming about Augusta National's linoleum-like, slippery, fast greens, she ordered —or stop playing in the Masters.

"She said, 'You'd better come back with a better attitude about putting, or why come back?'" Singh recalled.

Like any wise husband, Singh listened to his wife.

"Golf in Fiji is like cricket is over here," Singh explained.

Nevertheless, by the time Vijay was 15, he was one of the best golfers in the Pacific. He left home in 1980, at the age of 17, to pursue a professional career in Australia and Malaysia.

Suspended for two years because of a scoring controversy that Singh insists was merely a misunderstanding, Vijay—which means "victory" in Hindi—took a job in 1985 as the head pro at Keningau Club, in the middle of a Borneo rain forest.

There, Singh gave golf lessons to curious lumberjacks at a course that, during the monsoon season, was often cut off from the outside world for weeks at a time.

Singh and his wife lived in a one-bedroom flat, in 100-degree heat and drew their drinking water from a community well.

Calvin Peete, the second black man ever to play in the Masters, became the center of controversy in the rain-delayed 1983 Masters when he made comments that were perceived to be critical of the tournament.

Perhaps as a result, he shot an 87 on the third round "I lost count out there," Peete admitted.

President Dwight Eisenhower was a frequent and favored guest at Augusta National.

One afternoon, Ike and some of pals who were playing a leisurely round, were on the 15th green preparing to putt when a ball suddenly sailed into their midst.

Moments later, an elderly man walked briskly onto the green, informed the President and his friends that he was playing through, then proceeded to sink his putt and depart—without another word.

The rude intruder was baseball legend and Georgia native Ty Cobb.

In the early years, Augusta National often ran short of knowledgeable people to serve as rules officials on the various holes. One year, Bobby Jones' father, Colonel Bob Jones, was pressed into service on the final day of the tournament on the 12th hole.

It had rained overnight and there was standing water on the course. When a player hit a shot into a particularly soggy area near Rae's Creek, he asked the elder Jones if he was entitled to relief.

"Where do you stand in relation to par?" The Colonel inquired.

"Eighteen over," the golfer replied.

"Then what in the goddamn hell difference does it make?" Bob Jones Sr. wanted to know. "Tee the thing up on a peg for all I give a hoot!"

On the putting green at the 2000 Masters, Northern Ireland's Darren Clarke suddenly began sinking one six-foot-putt after another.

Clink. Clink. Ball after ball disappeared into the cup, with nary a miss. It was quite a performance.

From the other end of the practice green, Tiger Woods was watching intently. Finally, Tiger walked over and attempted to strike up a conversation with Clarke.

But Clarke purposely ignored him. Shut him out completely. Simply blocked the best player in the game out of his mind.

Gamesmanship.

"Everybody has got their own opinion about Tiger Woods," explained Clarke. "Unquestionably he's the best player in the world. But even the best player in the world isn't unbeatable. And from a personal point, I know that. I already beat him."

After Clarke upset Woods in Match Play Championship earlier that year, Darren, who is not exactly famous for his physical fitness, returned to the La Costa clubhouse, with his $1 million check in hand, to find a note tacked up in his locker.

It was from Woods.

"Well done, again," Tiger's message read. "But you're still a fat man."

More gamesmanship.

The late Payne Stewart played in his first Masters in 1983 and enjoyed two top-10 finishes—a tie for eighth in 1986 and a tie for ninth in '93.

But he never seemed comfortable at Augusta National. And he didn't try to hide his disdain for the greens, which he considered too fast.

"The Masters is my least favorite of the four majors," admitted Stewart, who sometimes wore a shirt and necktie in addition to his trademark knickers during the annual Par-3 Contest. "I don't think I'm ever going to figure this place out."

Fuzzy Zoeller whistles while he works. Bernhard Langer proceeds at a snail's pace. Lee Trevino won't shut up on the course. Ben Hogan used to stare.

With Swedish meatball Jesper Parnevik, it's the cap and the clothes that annually set him apart at Augusta.

They call him the "Spaceman," and not just because he turns up the bill of his cap like a golfing Gomer Pyle.

To the eccentric Parnevik, it made perfect sense in the beginning: He wanted to get some sun on his face.

The son of the most famous comedian in Sweden, Parnevik is a math whiz and has a photographic memory. He's read the Koran and has studied quantum mechanics. He speaks three languages: Swedish, English and German.

Thinking he had missed the cut, Parnevik once left a tournament. When he reached his hotel, he discovered he was one of four players tied for the final spot and eligible for a sudden-death playoff. By the time he scrambled back to the course, the playoff was over.

Parnevik once showed up in the wrong city for a tournament in his native Sweden. He lost his airplane ticket four times on the same trip. And more than once he has climbed into his car and driven away, without remembering to put his clubs in the trunk. He also has been known to forget what hotel he's staying at.

"I've done a lot of spacey things," Parnevik admitted.

At the 1999 Masters, an intrepid reporter asked the often stoic David Duval how it felt to be "a dullard."

"A what?" Duval demanded, his brow furrowed.

"A dullard," the reporter repeated.

"Is that your impression?" the obviously stunned Duval inquired.

"I don't know," the reporter, suddenly on the defensive, replied.

"If that's the perception, that's fine," Duval declared, folding his fingers beneath his chin. "That's how I try to play."

South African-born Nick Price was about to putt one year when an announcer in the nearby TV broadcast booth noted that the wind had suddenly changed directions.

"There was a gust of wind from Nick's rear just as he was about to putt," the announcer reported.

To which longtime CBS producer/director Frank Chirkinian, listening back in the control truck, responded:

"Did Nick have Mexican food last night?"

Doug Sanders grew up on a farm in rural Georgia and dreamed of someday playing in the Masters at Augusta National.

As Sanders recalled: "When I was a boy, my dad said, 'Son, when in hell are you ever going to grow up to be something? You could go work at the service station and make 50 cents an hour. But you're out on the golf course and that will never amount to anything.'"

When Sanders was 17, he made his first trip to Augusta, to play in a national junior qualifying tournament at Augusta Country Club, next door to Augusta National.

"We rode by Augusta National," Sanders recalled, "and I said, 'Man, oh man, someday I'm going to go on there and play.' "

Which, of course, he eventually did. To this day, Sanders, an annual regular at the Masters, even though he no longer competes, treasures a photo of himself, Jack Nicklaus and Arnold Palmer, walking off a tee together.

21

The Little Guy

"There were all these millions of people pulling for (Arnold) Palmer, and there I was, this little guy from South Africa, and only my wife and my dog were pulling for me."

— *Gary Player*

At the 1961 Masters, South Africa's Gary Player reached the par-3 16th hole very much in contention for the championship and a coveted green jacket.

As Player carefully studied his putt for par, he informed his caddie that he thought he ought to play the ball on the left edge of the cup.

"No, Mr. Player," the caddie protested. "It's right edge all the way."

When Player continued to disagree, the caddie said: "If you put it on the right edge and it doesn't go in, I'm working for free this week. And you know I can't afford that."

Impressed with his caddie's confidence, Player played the shot on the right edge and it dropped into the cup.

"It was the most important putt I made all week," Player admitted.

Gary Player was hardly the people's choice at Augusta in April of 1961. The galleries were all on Arnold Palmer's side. Augusta National, after all, was the birthplace of Arnie's Army.

As Player recalled: "There were all these millions of people pulling for Palmer, and there I was, this little guy from South Africa, and only my wife and my dog were pulling for me.

"It was understandable," Player acknowledged. "But I had a four-shot lead at one point and still many people say that Arnold Palmer blew it on the 72nd hole."

The South African-born Player, who became the first foreign-born Masters champion in 1961, was once a protégé of controversial, well-to-do early Masters amateur competitor Frank Stranahan, an avid body-builder.

"I taught him how to dress," the outspoken Stranahan once boasted. "Wear all black or all white, not like Arnold Palmer and all these other guys with no class."

Player is one of only six men in history to win as many as three Masters. Only his arch-rivals, Jack Nicklaus (six) and Arnold Palmer (four), have won more.

Player, who at age 62, became the oldest player ever to make the cut at the Masters in 1998, is also a fitness fanatic.

Which may explain why, despite the obvious physical advantages of many of his peers, he has been so successful for so long.

On the Sunday before his successful 1961 Masters, Player awoke in the middle of the night to find

Gary Player

the house which he and his family had rented in Augusta for the week on fire.

Player had tossed a carpet over a heater before going to bed that evening and it erupted in flames. Player awoke to find the house filled with smoke. "There was so much smoke I couldn't see my wife, lying in bed next to me," he said.

Fortunately, everyone escaped safely, although Player was slightly burned when he tried to stamp out the flames with his bare foot.

"We would have been dead in five minutes if I hadn't awakened," he admitted.

Leading the 1974 Masters by one shot as he played the 17th hole, Player, who was in the middle of the fairway at the time, informed his caddie: "We're not gonna putt here."

Player, the eventual champion, almost looked like a prophet when his 9-iron shot stopped just inches from the hole for an easy birdie that sealed the win.

In 1978, still weighing that same 150 pounds that he weighed when he won his first Masters title in 1961, 42-year-old Player set out to prove the power of physical fitness.

The little South African fired a final-round 64, including a sizzling 30 on the back nine, to overtake Rod Funseth, Hubert Green and Tom Watson and claim his third green jacket.

Gary Player had his tonsils removed in an Augusta hospital on the Monday before the 1964 Masters.

22

World's Wonder Inland Golf Course

"It is the most awe-inspiring feeling, to drive into the golf club, play the course, and take part in the tournament. It is a myth, but by that I don't mean it's a bunch of falsehoods, It's a believable, lovable myth."

— *Frank Beard*

Each of Augusta National's 18 picturesque holes is named for a flower or tree. And each hole on the course that designer Alister Mackenzie often called the "World's Wonder Inland Golf Course," has a history all its own.

As Bobby Jones explained in his book *Golf Is My Game*: "We want to make bogies easy if frankly sought, pars readily obtainable by standard good play, and birdies, except on par-5s, dearly bought."

The two nines were reversed after the inaugural Masters in 1934—the original first hole became the 10th hole, and vice versa—when Bobby Jones and Clifford Roberts discovered that, on frosty mornings, play could comfortably begin earlier in the day on what is now the front nine because it is located on higher ground.

That was actually the order Mackenzie first had in mind when he drew his initial design for Augusta National.

Augusta National underwent a total of 69 official course alterations during its first 67 years. But arguably the most significant series of changes were made prior to the 2002 Masters.

Under the supervision of house architect Tom Fazio, nine of the 18 holes were lengthened, adding nearly 300 yards to a course that already favored big hitters such as Tiger Woods.

The most dramatic change came on the critical 18th hole, which was lengthened to 465 yards with trouble on both sides of the fairway.

The 1st, 7th, 8th, 9th, 10th, 11th, 13th and 14th holes were all also lengthened.

Hole No. 1, "Tea Olive," Par 4, 435 yards:

"The first shot in any major championship is the most important one you'll hit," observed Jack Nicklaus, who knows a thing or two about what it takes to win a major championship.

Ill-fated Roberto De Vicenzo began the final round of the 1968 Masters by holing a 9-iron from 135 yards out for an eagle-2—the first such feat on the opening hole in 28 years.

Hole No. 2, "Pink Dogwood," Par 5, 575 yards:

Often eagled, but still the only par-5 at Augusta that has yet to yield a double-eagle.

Sam Snead and Craig Stadler both eagled this hole four times in their careers, and Gay Brewer (1970), Andy Bean (1977), Sam Torrance (1985) and Steve Jones (1990) eagled it twice in the same tournament.

Gardner Dickinson once proposed that the Masters airline office, which is located at the club to assist players in making last-minute changes in their travel plans, be moved into the ravine on the left side of the second fairway.

Dickinson argued that any player who drives his ball into the ravine might just as well begin making plans to go home.

Hole No. 3, "Flowering Peach," Par 4, 350 yards:

"No. 3 may be short, but it can eat your lunch," said two-time Masters champion Tom Watson. "This is one of the best short par-4s I've ever played."

As if to prove Watson's point, Tiger Woods hit his drive to within 15 yards of the green on the second round in 1997, but nevertheless bogeyed the hole.

Hole No. 4, "Flowering Crab Apple," Par 3, 205 yards:

Aced in 1992 by Jeff Sluman, who began his first round birdie-birdie-par-ace, this hole once featured a variety of palm trees. Only one remains.

Some residential power lines just outside the property were once visible beyond the green. But soon after the president of Georgia Power Co. was invited to join Augusta National in 1966, those power lines disappeared.

Hole No. 5, "Magnolia," Par 4, 435 yards:

The toughest hole on the course, in the opinion of Davis Love III—and also his personal favorite.

"You can talk about 'Amen Corner' (Nos. 11 through 13) all you want," said Love, "but 3, 4, 5 and 6 are the meat of the course. If you play these holes in 1 or 2 under, you're in good shape."

Jack Nicklaus, the all-time leader in Masters eagles (24) as well as green jackets (six) eagled this hole twice in 1995.

"In the first round, I hit a 5-iron into the middle of the green that rolled in," Jack explained, "On Sunday, I knocked in a 7-iron for my second 2."

Hole No. 6, "Juniper," Par 3, 180 yards:

Masters founder Bobby Jones was in his white cabin at Augusta National during the final round of the 1954 tournament when he heard a loud roar from one of the galleries out on the course.

"I'm willing to bet that Billy Joe Patton has done something unusual," Jones declared.

Indeed, he had. Using a 5-iron, Patton became the first golfer to ace the sixth hole in tournament play.

Hole No. 7, "Pampas," Par 4, 410 yards:

Originally considered the weakest hole at Augusta, Jack Nicklaus now calls this "one of the great little short holes in golf.

"Any time you can walk away with a birdie, you feel you've gained a stroke on the field," Nicklaus declared.

Larry Mize, who eagled the hole in 1999, played it in 4-under-par during the 1994 Masters to tie the tournament record set by Sam Snead in 1957 when he birdied the hole four days in a row.

Hole No. 8, "Yellow Jasmine," Par 5, 570 yards:

Bruce Devlin recorded the one and only double eagle here in 1967.

"If I believe everybody who comes up to me and tells me they saw it, there must have been 10,000 people there," Devlin said.

In fact, the gallery around the green numbered only about 1,500 when Devlin struck his first-round 4-wood shot from the right side of the fairway.

Hole No. 9, "Carolina Cherry," Par 4, 460 yards:
In 1980, 25-year-old Curtis Strange, playing in just his second Masters, holed a 6-iron shot.

Six years later, en route to his sixth green jacket, Jack Nicklaus was preparing to putt when he heard a roar behind him on the eighth hole where Seve Ballesteros and Tom Kite had both holed pitch shots for eagles.

Turning to the gallery, Nicklaus calmly said, "Okay, let's see if we can make a roar of our own here."

Hole No. 10, "Camellia," Par 4, 495 yards:
Reigning U.S. Amateur Public Links champion Guy Yamamoto opened the 1995 Masters with an unsightly first-round 84. The next day, however, he knocked his second shot on the 10th hole, a 7-iron from 171 yards away, into the cup for a beautiful eagle.

Hole No. 11, "White Dogwood," Par 4, 490 yards:
The start of Augusta's storied "Amen Corner," normally short-hitting Jerry Barber recorded the lone Masters eagle here in 1962.

But that was overshadowed by Larry Mize's successful 140-foot chip shot on the second hole of his 1987 sudden death playoff.

"If you ever see me on the 11th green in two," Ben Hogan once remarked, "you'll know I missed my second shot."

Originally, a small pot bunker which could not be seen from tee was located in the middle of the 11th fairway.

In 1932, when Bobby Jones's father, Colonel Bob Jones, played the newly opened course for the first time, he unexpectedly found his tee shot in the sand.

Bellowed the elder Jones: "What goddamned fool put a goddamned bunker right in the goddamned center of the goddamned fairway?"

"I did," son Bobby replied.

Hole No. 12, "Golden Bell," Par 3, 155 yards:

Tom Watson calls this the most pivotal hole on the course. "Your whole round can swing on that hole," he noted. "And many have."

Curtis Strange was so excited when he aced this hole in 1998 that he pulled his ball out of the cup and hurled it into nearby Rae's Creek.

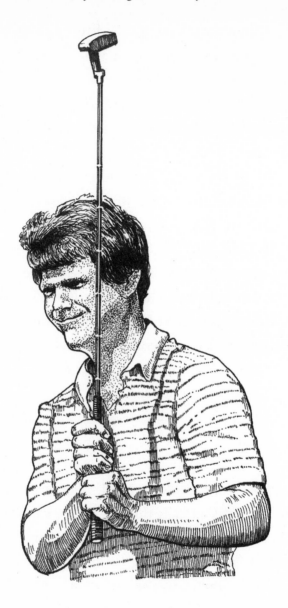

Tom Watson

"I threw the ball into the water to try to show some personality," Strange later explained. "But some of the writers crucified me for it. Somebody said I should have given it to my sons. Hopefully, I'll have something a little more important to give than a golf ball."

Hole No. 13, "Azalea," Par 5, 510 yards:

Larry Mize called this "the most fun hole out there." No doubt, Jeff Maggert would agree.

In 1994, after playing poorly all week, Maggert knocked his 3-iron second shot into the cup from 222 yards away on the final round.

"I was out so early there weren't a lot of people there to see it," Maggert admitted.

Dentist Cary Middlecoff sank a 75-foot second round eagle putt here en route to the 1955 championship.

Hole No. 14, "Chinese Fir," Par 4, 440 yards:

This is a hole Dan Pohl will never forget.

In 1982, Pohl sank a 118-yard wedge shot for an eagle on the third round of the tournament in the midst of an eagle-eagle-birdie-birdie run that eventually helped catapult him into a playoff with Craig Stadler.

"What do you have to do to win this thing?" Stadler asked his wife, as he headed for the 10th tee and the sudden-death showdown.

Stadler quickly found out as he birdied the first extra hole to win the playoff.

Hole No. 15, "Firethorn," Par 5, 500 yards:

To this day, Gene Sarazen's 1935 double eagle here remains one of the most celebrated shots, both in Masters and in golf history.

"The 15th hole represents the last real chance for a eagle," Tom Watson explained, "so you often fire for the green in two down the stretch."

Bruce Crampton eagled this hole on both the third and fourth rounds in 1974. Crampton also eagled No. 13 on the first round and No. 3 on the fourth round to set a Masters record that year.

Hole No. 16, "Redbud," Par 3, 170 yards:

Jack Nicklaus' sank a 50-foot putt here enroute to victory in 1975.

In 1986, with another green jacket—and what Nicklaus would later label his most memorable Masters championship—within his grasp, he hit a 5-iron to the green instead of his customary 6-iron.

"I remember my son, Jackie, saying after I hit it, 'Be enough, be enough,'" Nicklaus recalled.

"I turned to him, winked, and said, 'It is.'"

Hole No. 17, "Nandina," Par 4, 425 yards:

This hole, home to the famed Eisenhower Tree, was decisive in both of Tom Watson's Masters championships so it's understandable he has "fond memories" of this hole.

After Bernhard Langer birdied the 17th in 1985 to grab a commanding two-shot lead, his playing partner, Seve Ballesteros tapped him on the shoulder and said, "You deserve this one."

Hole No. 18, "Holly," Par 4, 465 yards:

In 1963, as Jack Nicklaus approached the green of this famed finishing hole, he glanced up at the scoreboard to check on his status and noticed a "2" alongside his name.

But he also saw several players with the number "1."

"I'm red-green color blind," Nicklaus explained, so I asked my caddie, Willie Peterson, how many of them were red (under par).

"He said, 'Just you, boss.'"

Epilogue

By Robert Hartman

It's venerable.

It's a pastoral picnic made up of an artist's palette that offers hues that expand beyond conceptual radiance.

It begins with 61 magnolia trees on a 330-yard drive up aptly named Magnolia Lane.

The heritage of the course and the Masters Tournament ebb into a modicum of *Can you believe it?* It's as much about the legacy of the course as it is about the sights, the sounds, and the smell of Augusta.

But, when the last putt drops, when the last azalea bud says goodnight, the understated elegance of the Augusta canvas becomes dormant in a way that it simply readies itself for the next performance. And, the tournament known simply as the Masters has become a sports rite of passage for as much as anything, the time of year. No event in America's culture has such a singular unveiling with nature. And no event measures it's success better by doing things within a tradition born in the spirit of a golf tournament, wound tightly by years and years of making the event a little better each year.

Two men, Bobby Jones and Clifford Roberts, founded Augusta National Golf Club. They thought it would be enterprising to allow gentlemen from across the nation an opportunity to join a club in the south that offers a place to commune. They met in the mid–1920s. Jones was the ambassador of a game and was a learned man off the fairways, having earned degrees from Emory University, Georgia Tech, and Harvard. Roberts had early success on Wall Street and he came to the club like a potter molding clay. He was an unassuming, bold perfectionist. They did not ignore the dollar; it was just merely not the most important aspect of their path. Together, they ushered a club, and eventually a golf tournament, into perfect harmony. There was a synergy that eventually made a large plat of land in Northwest Georgia a haven for golfing purists. Sure, there was a symbiotic old boys' network to building Augusta, and it still exists. Yet, some of the building blocks had to do with typical growth of an event and the cultural ties they were crossing. However, even before Rae's Creek became a water hazard for golf balls, and even before the first player said a prayer at Amen Corner, these two pioneers began to set the table. They enveloped a golf tournament around a pristine setting and a green jacket: simply a place and a prize.

The setting was clearly defined by nature. Roberts, Jones, and course designer Dr. Alister Mackenzie were aware of the unbridled pastoral elements of the land. And they did not force change on the golf course or the club; they just allowed it to evolve.

California's Cypress Point, its majestic vistas and the Monterey Peninsula, was the artistic and competitive standard in the 1920s. Cypress Point's reputation was one reason Jones sought Mackenzie's guile of design to the Georgia plantation. The collaboration of Robert and Jones, coupled with the endearing natural elements proved providential. Mackenzie brought to life a game-full test that was "playable." It was in 1933 that the course opened amid overcast skies and rain showers. Jones, who was at this time the winner of 13 championships, shot an opening round 69. Shortly after the club was christened, Jones began fading from tournament competition and his design was to implement a tournament that would challenge the Gene Sarazens and the Horton Smiths. Jones' grand slam run as competitive golfer was eventually exhausted by a neurological condition called syringomyelia.

But, the Masters we know today really began long before Jones, Roberts, and Mackenzie discovered it. The seed was planted by the Berckmans, the original owners of the land, for the large oak tree behind the clubhouse. The seed figuratively represents more than a natural landmark for the club. The branches, knots, bark and angles sweeping outward and skyward, still stands today. It represents the tales, the turns, and the steady growth pattern of an event. The Masters is successful for the same reason many players fold their tent on Sundays. It's revered as a classic, like an old hickory stick that has been preserved with layers of varnish. This is one of the few sporting spectacles that grew from the inside, the same as the live oak. Jones' and Roberts' endeavors were born in this same metaphor of taking root.

In 1934, the Augusta National Invitational began. It would soon become known as the Masters and remains an exclusive invitational only event. In 1937, Sam Snead was the first to be awarded a significant piece of apparel for the championship—a green jacket. The winner's check is modest in relationship to the money on the PGA Tour. But, it is within the thread of the green single-breasted blazer that buries the shoulders of the winner, that has become the tournament's signature prize. The testimony to what Jones and Roberts built is in the simplicity with which it has unraveled. "I'll take a 43-long," Phil Mickelson said after his 2010 Masters triumph.

The jacket is the symbol of golf, like the yellow jersey represents the Tour De France. The jacket is spilled over shoulders in the same genre a carafe of milk has become a part of the Indianapolis 500. The green sport jacket is iconic just as the Lombardi Trophy has come to symbolize the Super Bowl. And it is this quest to become fitted in this trademark apparel that has brought storylines, like when Jack Nicklaus journeyed through Amen Corner in 1986. For as many players who have challenged Augusta National, it was the one year that athletic accomplishment was reduced to a sentimental tug of generations. At the age of 46, the Golden Bear made a charge through Amen Corner that sent chills across generational lines. Nicklaus, in the twilight of his career, with his son as his caddie, rallied one last time. His sixth green jacket could be summarized in what founder Jones once said about the Golden Bear, "Jack Nicklaus is playing an entirely different game, and one which I'm not familiar with." For many years it was Jones who slipped the coat over the shoulders of the champion.

Comparing Augusta to any other sport would be a crucible, but not for the reasons that an average golf enthusiast would specter. Augusta is a picnic compared to the masses at other majors. There is a decorum that befits the event. Jones was ardent in his admonition that patrons not be hurried in their observance of the game. Leaving his stamp on the tournament, Jones wrote in 1967, "In golf, customs of etiquette and decorum are just as important as the rules governing play." Some would argue it's too controlled. Overzealous fans are not Augusta. Some have described the patrons at Augusta to be too polite and generally mannerly in their appreciation for well-hit small white spheres. And for under five dollars you can buy a pimento cheese sandwich, a bag of chips, and a cold soda. Where at major sporting venues can a fan walk up to a concessionaire and have a meal for that coin?

A picture taken every year at the Champions Dinner on Tuesday night of Masters week is simply a snapshot of golf's last hundred years.

Much like the early days with Roberts and Jones, Augusta and the Masters have gone through burgeoning growth patterns. About the time two midwestern golfers came on the scene, one that went to Ohio State with a steely-eyed determination and the other a swashbuckling Wake Forest grad. It was on their watch that Augusta became paved in green. And, it was in the 1960s and 1970s that the course made strides to becoming a monochromatic green pasture. The advent of turf equipment created a landscape that made bird's chirp with unbridled glee and the Masters committee enchanted like the seven dwarfs going to work on a tournament that was becoming increasingly visible. It became manicured in an ostentatious way. Thick rough, challenging the advancement of the golf ball is not Augusta. Unfair pin placements are not Augusta. Everything at Augusta is presented in an alarmingly straightforward manner. To hear the players bark about Augusta is fodder at the nuances of the game. The Masters is so much about minimizing mistakes and miscalculations. Players are charged with getting the ball into the hole in the fewest amount of strokes just the way Jones subscribed to the notion that, "Golf is really about turning three strokes into two." For example, the aerodynamic wind swirls at the par-three 12th are sometimes judged by the flagstick on the 11th green. Some have called the lengthening of the course over the past ten years Tiger-proofing. But, that discussion is not affecting results on the leaderboard. Ironically, the Masters has kept pace with the professional game in the way it has expanded its field to a larger pool of international players. Proof is in the recent winners like Angel Cabrera (Argentina), and South Africans Trevor Immelman and Charl Schwartzel.

The Masters has been the green theater for similar combatants to what we witnessed with Nicklaus and Palmer. Tiger Woods and Phil Mickelson, two gravitating personalities whittled from different persimmon, have led the patron shouting at Amen Corner over the last ten years. At first there were whispers about the left-hander's inability to clear the green jacket threshold. His break through in 2004 was one year removed from Tiger Woods winning back-to-back in 2001 and 2002. When Mickelson finally broke through he said, "In the past ten years I have come so close, so many times, to have had good last rounds fall short, and to have bad last rounds and fall short. To have such a difficult journey to win my first major, makes it that much sweeter." But, even after Chris DiMarco gave him a perfect read on his decisive putt on the 18th green, he tried to put into context his emotions. "I don't know what to say, to tell you how awesome it feels. It just feels so good, but I don't think any Masters will ever compare to the '86 Masters. But, for me this one does."

In 2005, the Masters came down to a battle between DiMarco and Woods. It was on the edge of the 16th green, staring at a bogey when he chipped his ball high on the crest of the slope and the golfing world watched the Nike ball roll increasingly closer to the cup, one rotation after another until it finally crashed into golfdom. Woods defined the last rotations, "Somehow an earthquake happened and it fell in the hole."

Other amazing shots are part of Masters lore. Mickleson's six-iron off the pine straw at 13 in the 2010 tournament led to him winning his third green jacket in a similar sword-waggling way. After the defining shot he quipped, "A great shot is when you pull it off. A smart shot is when you don't have the guts to try it." And, at the end of the decade, the tally had been erased and reedified. Woods and Mickelson each earned three wins in the decade.

Woods' first, in 1997, the proclaimed victory for the ages still rattles the pines on the old Berckman's land.

Somewhere in the champions locker room there is a tally sheet, Woods four, Mickelson three.

To reduce the Masters to Nicklaus, Palmer, Mickelson, and Woods would be similar to reducing the Kentucky Derby to Secretariat and Seattle Slew. But, through the generations of the tournament and the champions, there have been memorable shots, comebacks, and of course, collapses. To put Rory Mcllroy's back nine debacle in 2010 into context is daunting. So many players have felt a similar pain. Scott Hoch in a playoff in 1989, and of course Greg Norman's horror show in 1996. Mcllroy's final round lead was painfully whittled away by the time he left Amen Corner. But, the late Herbert Warren Wind would have had trouble eloquently describing the misfortune of the young lad from Northern Ireland. The Mcllroy final round 80 was strikingly similar to Greg Norman's back nine circus in 1996. But, just as Nick Faldo seized the moment that year, something that had never happened at Augusta occurred last year. Charl Schwartzel became the first Masters Champion to birdie the last four holes.

The vernacular of the Masters is somewhat Jim Nantzian. His Cal Ripken-like 27-year run continues at Augusta. Somehow the singular word that simply rises to the top like the dew on the greens is—*tradition*. Nantz's "A tradition unlike any other" has aptly introduced not just an event, but also a sport. Nantz first called action at Augusta in 1986 at the bequest of CBS's Frank Chirkinian (who passed on in 2011). It was his call, "The Bear has come out of hibernation," which followed the Nicklaus birdie at 16 on Sunday. And, between the 1997 call of Tiger Woods'; "One for the ages." Or in 2010, when Mickelson triumphed to the Nantz proclamation "One for the family."

Tradition is the live oak. Tradition is the pimento cheese and the green patron chairs that line the fairways. Tradition is Magnolia Lane, the green jacket, and Butler Cabin. Tradition is the players skipping the ball over the 16th pond during practice rounds. Tradition is the groans and exultations at Amen corner. Tradition is the now televised Par-three event. Tradition is the white caddie smocks and the ceremonial tee-shot by the legends of the game (beginning in 1963) off the first tee on Thursday. Tradition is the logo. Tradition is the U.S. Amateur Champion playing with the previous year's champion. Tradition is the cabana seating area behind the clubhouse. Unmistakably, tradition is the amateur's quarters called the Crow's Nest and players playing in twosomes.

But, tradition is not something you can smell. Tradition is representative of what the tournament has become. Yet, one of the most compelling aspects of Augusta is the smell of fresh cut grass. It's the smell of the pines and the smell of the flowers with outstretched petals. Another aspect to Augusta that slowly made its way through the tapestry of technology is the hills. The golf course is not a flat pastured goat ranch. There is a traversing vertical challenge to playing the course that is unmistaken on an outsider's first recognition of Augusta.

I can remember the first time I set foot on the grounds and walked from the media center out to the first fairway. Looking across the great green divide is simply majestic in all things green. But, what is equally striking is the elevation changes. There is a serenity and calmness to the arena. For all the golf played at Augusta, the one shot that is still embedded in my soul is the tee shot from Fred Couples on the par-three 12th in the 1992 Masters. It is somewhat mystical how the ball defied the gravitational yearning of Rae's Creek. The other tournament that is memorable is Ben Crenshaw's second green jacket in 1995. Crenshaw talked about how he was led around Augusta National by the memory of Harvey Penick, who had died one week prior to the tournament. The emotion of grieving for his long time teacher and applying the wit and wisdom was evident by Crenshaw as he finished the tournament cradled in the arms of his caddie Carl Jackson. In *Harvey Penick's Little Red Book*, noted University of North Carolina sports psychologist Dick Coop said, "Harvey Penick teaches (golf) in parables." And, the best way to describe the Masters is that it's an sporting event where a new parable is often written every second week of April. It's simply part of the tradition.

Bibliography

Brown, Cal. (1998). *Masters Moments.* Sleeping Bear Press.

Editors of *Golf Magazine.* (1997). *Tall Tales of Golf.* Triumph Books.

Eubanks, Steve. (1997). *Augusta.* Broadway Books.

Feinstein, John. (1999). *The Majors.* Little, Brown and Company.

Green, Ron. (2001). *Shouting at Amen Corner.* Sports Publishing, LLC.

McCord, Gary. (1997). *Just a Range Ball in a Box of Titleists.* G.P. Putnam's Sons.

Morrison, Ian. (1987). *Great Moments in Golf.* Gallery Books.

Morrison Ian. (1988). *100 Greatest Golfers.* Crescent Books.

Owen, David. (1999). *The Making of the Master.* Simon and Schuster.

Peper, George. (1991). *Grand Slam Golf.* Henry N. Abrams.

Sampson, Curt. (1999). *The Masters.* Villard Books.

Silverman, Jeff. (2001). *The Greatest Golf Stories Ever Told.* Lyons Press.

Snead, Sam. (1997). *The Game I Love.* Ballantine Books.

Towle, Mike. (2000). *I Remember Augusta.* Cumberland House Publishing.

Wade, Don. (2001). *Talking on Tour.* Contemporary Books.

Wind, Herbert Warren. (1985). *Following Through.* Ticknor & Fields.

Wright, Ben. (1999). *Good Bounces and Bad Lies.* Sleeping Bear Press.